ALMOST THERE

Stories and Musings
along the Pacific Crest Trail

G. William Jolley

Copyright © 2014 G. William Jolley

ISBN-13: 978-1508418900

ISBN-10: 150841890X

For Carla Maria Jolley

Who Stayed

ACKNOWLEDGEMENTS

I have yet to read a book written by committee. Books are written in the solitude of one's study, the quiet corner of home, or, as is often the case, in the backrooms of local coffee houses or libraries. And yet, no matter what the author's process, a book worth its salt is touched by many hands and comes under the scrutiny and guidance of trusted friends, colleagues, and editors at assorted times within the process of writing. I have all these to thank and acknowledge:

From the first page to the last, I have my longstanding writing partner to thank. Adrian (Dick) Magnuson's patient and faithful input and editorial counsel was more than any writer could ever ask for.

To Katherine Flannigan, who suffered through the first draft and accomplished the hard work of paring-down all the redundancies and wretched syntactical errors.

To Lynn Willeford, whose critical editorial skills and vision gave me confidence that I had actually written a book worthy of publication.

To Sarah Mackaman, Molly Brewer, and Carla Jolley, who read the penultimate draft and offered invaluable feedback of how to make this book clearer and more interesting.

And to Audrey Mackaman, whose final edit readied this book for publication.

To all of you I am grateful beyond expression and shout-out my deepest thanks. You were my "committee," without whom this book would never be completed. To you all, I owe an extraordinary debt.

I acknowledge all the Trail Angels and assorted PCT hikers I encountered along the Washington section of the Pacific Crest Trail. Most I knew only by their "trail names," but all had a significant part in making my experience rich and remarkable. I am filled with deep gratitude for your presence in my life during those weeks on the Trail. Some of you kept me from harm's way, others simply encouraged me to continue, a few laughed at my horrible jokes, and some shared campsites and campfires. We often told our own stories, shared our passions and dreams with abandon and vulnerability, and in so doing, we enriched one another. You have all filled my life with wonderful, memorable, funny, and tender stories. I will remember you all with fondness and an occasional smile.

CONTENTS

Old men ought to be explorers,

Here and there does not matter

We must be still and still moving

Into another intensity

For further union, a deeper communion

Through the dark cold and the empty desolation...

T.S. Eliot

PROLOGUE

I never imagined my life would pass by so quickly, almost in a blink of an eye. How did I get to seventy so soon? Was I not paying attention? I thought I was, but when I look into a mirror I don't see the young man I feel I am. There's an old man staring back at me. Tolstoy was correct to claim that the biggest surprise in a man's life is old age. So I suppose one of my motives for hiking hundreds of miles along the Pacific Crest Trail was to prove that an old man could hike some of the most rugged trails anywhere in the United States. Vanity? Ego? Perhaps. Yet what better way to celebrate life and health than to go into the wilderness and hike alone, carrying on my back only what was essential? But was I too late?

Hiking the Pacific Crest Trail was an elaborate extension of nearly sixty years of a love affair with the wilderness. I concur with John Muir, who claimed that if we don't foster a relationship and link to the wilderness, we risk losing our own humanity. In the wilderness, we not only have the opportunity to rediscover parts of ourselves long dormant, but we also have the possibility to witness creation at its most raw and most remarkable. But less poetically, I undertook this adventure to prove that the wilderness is also for old men and not simply the young and frisky. Indeed, old men ought to be explorers, still moving into another intensity.

All motives are mixed and there is seldom a straight and clear line from conception to action. But one thing I am certain about is that I did not hike the Pacific Crest Trail to discover myself. I wasn't lost. Nor did I embark on this experience to find meaning or purpose. I don't believe meaning is to be found. Rather, it is something we make or create out of the raw materials that life gives us. And I did not hike hundreds of miles on the Pacific Crest Trail in the course of two summers to sort out any tragedy or crisis in my life, real or existential. And even if that were so, a trek into the wilderness would not fill a hole in my soul. Neither would booze or sex or money or accolades. I know. I've tried them all.

There is something about being alone in the wilderness that is seductive and compelling, rich and extraordinary. In the wilderness there are no judgments. I seem to have become increasingly invisible with age. Hiking the Pacific Crest Trail spoke to some of my most desperate needs to belong and connect with something larger and vaster than myself. On the trail, I was not merely an old man walking alone. There, I had presence and was visible.

THE PATHS TAKEN

For two consecutive summers, 2012 and 2013, I hiked sections of the Pacific Crest Trail. The total mileage was close to 1,300 miles, and aside from an occasional encounter with other Pacific Crest Trail hikers or a smattering of day hikers, I hiked alone. In 2012 I was seventy years old. The average age of most hikers I met was early twenties to early thirties. On the Trail, I could claim being the oldest by two generations.

The trek in 2012 was the Washington section that stretches from the Bridge of the Gods at the Oregon/Washington border to the Washington/Canada border. The second trek was the Oregon section, where I began in Dunsmuir, California and finished at the Columbia Gorge, just yards from where I had begun the previous summer. Both summers I began in August and hiked for about six weeks, finishing in mid-September. But this book is an account of my trek along the Washington section in August and September 2012.

The Pacific Crest Trail (hereafter referred to as the PCT) is a 2,700-mile pathway that stretches from the Mexican border at Compos to the Canadian border, where PCT hikers officially end at Manning Park in British Columbia. The Trail passes through twenty-four national forests, seven state parks, and seven national parks. Along the PCT, hikers are treated to unobstructed, bold, and breathtaking views of Mt. Adams, Mt. Hood, Mt. Jefferson, Mt. St. Helens, Mt. Rainier, Glacier Peak, and a host of equally beautiful and magnificent mountains, meadows, and valleys. Moreover, the PCT hiker passes by, through, and over lakes, streams, and rivers too numerous to recount. Within the course of his journey, the PCT hiker who completes the entire trail will pass through six out of the seven North American ecozones, and for those who pay close attention, there is a point on the Trail where a hiker crosses the forty-fifth latitude line that lies midway between the equator and the North Pole. On the evening I camped at that spot, I lit a cigar in celebration. It seemed an important milestone in my life as a backpacker.

Those who hike the entire trail from end to end are referred to as "thru hikers." Typically, they begin in late April or early May at Compos, California and hike from south to north. In the two summers I hiked the Washington and Oregon sections, I met only a handful of PCT hikers who began in Canada to hike southward towards Compos.

Those who opt for a specific section of the trail rather than its entirety are referred to as "section hikers." Upon meeting a hiker along the trail, one is commonly and straightaway asked, "You a thru hiker or doing a section?" I was among the latter, and both in the Washington and Oregon sections, I chose to hike from south to north.

The reader will soon discover this account is not merely about the PCT. It is neither a guidebook nor a thorough description of the many miles of trail I hiked. There are better books for those purposes. Rather, I write only a few of my most notable experiences to offer the reader some insight into my journey. In a way, I wrote about this experience so I would always remember I had actually accomplished what I set out to do. But this book is larger than that. It is also about my life, my thoughts, my reflections, and my memories of past events, relationships, and experiences. In the end, it is a record of an exceptional experience for those who matter most in my life.

Writing a memoir is a curiously mixed endeavor. To tolerate life, we must be moving forward and beyond our past. In a way, each day we reinvent ourselves. Yet memoir is about looking back and reflecting on what once occurred, or at least how we remember what occurred. In so doing, we are pulled back into places and memories we have put behind us in order to move forward. In the very act of writing, we unravel those well-guarded memories and make choices about what to include and what to leave at rest. The Alcoholics Anonymous Program uses the pithy maxim, "You can look back but not stare." Eight to ten hours of hiking each day gave me ample time to look back and reflect on past events, some with more intensity than others. Some with humor, and some with sadness and regret. And with the hours and days and weeks of solo hiking, I remembered things I hadn't thought of or spoken about for decades. Some of what bubbled to consciousness caused me to shake my head and wonder how I managed to get from there to here. Some memories had a heartbeat, though often faint, while others weren't worth resuscitating.

Hiking the Washington section of the PCT was an experience of wonder and inexplicable beauty that surrounded me every day, providing the opportunity to open my mind and heart to my past. This is an account of that journey.

1

THE FIRST STEPS

A person brings to the Trail who he is. Not even deep into the wilderness, away from all accountability and notice, can one escape oneself. No matter who you are or where you come from, no matter how clever or bold, you cannot out-hike who you are. I suppose there is always the possibility and opportunity to reinvent oneself, but even then, eventually we return to who we are and where we began. That said, a certain level of confidence and experience is warranted and needed to hike the PCT. Hundreds of miles of solo hiking is, indeed, a daunting challenge. And no matter how much experience or how many years in the mountains, no one can know everything that needs knowing about long-distance backpacking. This in itself is the fundamental lesson and the truth of it. Some believe they know more than others and some think they know enough to get them where they want to go. But it's risky business to enter any wilderness area with more hubris than common sense. Some claim that risky behavior is a rite of passage, especially for men. But risk combined with arrogance is a fatal brew. I began with intentional caution.

With that in mind, on a clear, hot Sunday afternoon, July 29, 2012, following a killer brunch in Portland with my wife, Carla, and our daughter, Paige, Carla and I drove east on Highway 84 towards the Columbia River Gorge. Once at the Gorge, we drove across the Bridge of the Gods that spans the Columbia River into Washington State. An immediate left once off the bridge and another hundred yards down the road brought us to the sign that designated where the PCT trailhead began for the Washington section. At 180 feet above sea level, I was starting at the lowest elevation along the PCT. At first glance it seemed I had caught a break from too arduous a trek on my first day. In fact, almost immediately the trail began an upward ascent that took nearly three days of strenuous hiking before it ever leveled out.

Carla pulled the car over to the side of the road and turned off the motor. We sat silently staring forward through the windshield for nearly a full minute before she broke the thickness of the silence.

"You don't have to go, you know."

"Oh, yes I do," I said quietly, still looking forward out the windshield. "Besides, I've told too many people that I'm doing this."

"'Pride cometh before the fall,' you often say."

She turned to me with a broad smile. I thought how much I would miss that smile and then opened the car door. Within a few seconds we were standing at the back of the car with the trunk wide open, exposing my backpack that seemed to fill the entire trunk space. I hadn't remembered it being so huge when I'd crammed it into the trunk that morning.

"My God," I said, "how the hell will I ever hike with that boulder on my back?"

"Stop with the exaggerating. It looks more like a big rock." She shook her head and laughed to herself. "Well," she said, "you'll just have to eat a lot of food before it gets any lighter."

True and obvious, my pack *should* get lighter as I ate through the provisions. And by the time I collected my first reload box at Trout Lake, sixty miles north, it would be a reasonable expectation that my pack would be several pounds lighter.

I hoisted the "big rock" from the trunk space and swung it onto my back. My knees buckled, and right away I sensed my pack was about ten to fifteen pounds overweight. But the die, as they say, was cast, and around 2:00 p.m., with about six hours of daylight left in the day, I kissed Carla one last time, had her take my picture standing next to the PCT signage at the trailhead, and with a beating heart of trepidation took the first steps heading north out of the Columbia Gorge towards the Canadian border about five hundred miles away. I did not look back to watch Carla drive over the bridge and west towards home. Though we would speak over the phone at various points along the trail when I collected a reload box, I would not see her again for nearly six weeks.

Though I had studied the maps with avid attention for two months before leaving, somehow I had not absorbed the fact that the hike out of the Columbia Gorge was nearly three days of switchbacks and difficult miles of severe elevation. And that first day, as I hiked up and up and up, I knew this would be a short mileage day. Within an hour into the day, I decided I would camp at Gillette Lake, a small body of water about seven miles away and barely noticeable on the map. It looked to be situated just a few yards off the Trail with a couple of possible campsites. Given a late start on the first day, seven miles would be sufficient.

I reached Gillette Lake around 6:00 p.m. I had had enough for one day—a mere seven miles and yet my body felt as though I had covered about twenty. Screw it, I thought. This was not a test, no one was keeping score, and I was not accountable to anyone for how well I did on any given day. This was my hike, my experience, and I could set the rules. Hell, I didn't even have to finish the thing.

I removed The Rock, dropped it at my feet on the sandy ground, took out my stove, and boiled a couple cups of water I'd scooped from the lake. And as I sat waiting for the water to boil for my evening tea, I perused the map to see what the next day would require. It was a routine I pretty much followed each and every day of the hike: Around 6:00 p.m. or 7:00 p.m. I would start thinking about ending the day near a water source, settle on a space to pitch the tent, remove my boots, boil water for a cup of tea, calculate how far I had hiked that day, look to see where I was going the next day, and take a few minutes to write in my journal. The watch I brought with me only told the time of day, so I figured that the only way I could stay true to the days and dates was to write each day in the journal. I simply had to be certain that the first day in the journal was accurate and the rest would follow.

That cup of tea on that first evening tasted especially good. It was a celebration that I had actually begun the Trail, had fired up my stove for my first meal, and acknowledged that I was an authentic PCT hiker. All the months of planning and preparing, purchasing, and packing had brought me to this very moment.

So, with two teaspoons of sugar added to the tea and with cup in hand, I sat on the sandy ground with my back leaned against a log and watched three herons catch fish from the lake. They didn't seem to mind that I was a witness to their activity. Then, with fish in their long beaks, they flew off towards some distant place across the lake to savor their catch. I wondered: If I had been sitting at that very spot a thousand years ago, would I be witness to the same thing? It is likely that the great blue heron hasn't changed much over a millennium. They look so prehistoric; I wondered how they had missed the rest of their species' evolution.

After a second cup of tea, I began unpacking the entire backpack to find my tent and sleeping bag and all the things I would need for dinner. This was my first dinner on the PCT, so I selected my favorite package of dehydrated food...Mountain House beef stew. Two cups of boiling water into the package, a ten-minute wait, and presto! Dinner is served, along with a couple tortillas. For dessert I devoured a Pay Day candy bar. I had packed one for each of the next six days.

After dinner I put away my cooking paraphernalia and found a flat area about ten feet from the lake's edge, pitched my one-person tent, blew up the sleeping pad, unfolded the sleeping bag, then scooted in. It was about 8:30 p.m. and still light, but the end of the day for me. I whispered a quick prayer of gratitude and fell asleep.

***

On the morning of the Day Two, I awoke at sunrise and lay in my tent listening to a nearby gurgling brook. It took me another hour to scoot out and fire up my stove to boil some water for my inaugural cup of wretched instant coffee. I considered next what could be a significant contribution to humanity: someone inventing an instant coffee that was reasonably drinkable. I'm not asking for much here. Just something that is a bit tastier than Folgers Crystals. Fortunately, I brought ample sugar, and I loaded it into my cup.

A word about this cup. I could have purchased a cup adequate for this adventure at any local hardware store or garage sale for about ten cents. But earlier that summer, as I meandered up and down the aisles of our local REI, my eye caught a glimpse of this most remarkable shiny cup, and I snatched it up, absolutely believing it promised an exceedingly more valuable camping experience as long as I was willing to pay the twelve-dollar asking price. According to my youngest son, Jonah, I'm an "REI whore." To this date, I have not told Jonah of my purchase. Sometimes it's a bit unnerving to acknowledge the insights of a youngest son, even when I know he is right.

By the time I finished my breakfast of instant oatmeal covered with raisins and honey and repacked my pack, it was already 8:00 a.m. For some inexplicable reason, I had locked into a compulsion to be on the trail around 7:00 a.m., but it seemed there were endless, piddly things that required attending to before I could begin.

Sometime between breakfast and taking the first step of the day's hike, I made it a part of my routine to sit for a few minutes and read something from the pocket New Testament/Psalms I had packed. Mostly I read something from the Psalms to give me a kernel of inspiration and to remind me that this experience was one of trust and thankfulness. Those early minutes of reading and meditation were worth the time. They put clarity and gratitude into my heart and mind. That first morning I didn't leave my campsite until after 8:30 a.m. In the weeks that followed, I had met several other PCT hikers, all of whom told me they were typically on the trail between 5:00 a.m. and 6:00 a.m. Compared to their schedule, I was a slacker. But I had no imperative or accountability on my own time. I loved the idea of such simplicity.

On this first morning, I felt rested and optimistic. The sky was clear blue, the air was crisp, and the sun was already warming the air. I deemed it a perfect day for a hike.

Again, no one was watching or taking score or waiting for me to clock in. What I did each day or when I began or how many breaks I decided to take or what rock I chose to sit on or how long I desired to look out at a valley or mountain or how many minutes I stared into a cool, clear stream of water was purely and utterly within my control. But right then I felt an imperative to get up and get moving. Once more, old mental tapes of being responsible or keeping busy played in my head. But I wanted to keep in mind that I would never pass this way again, so every mile, every day, would be a special one. I wanted to find a way to make peace with that fact. No one, except me, would make these decisions. I needed to remember each and every day to be kind to myself. To be patient. To be forgiving. I would think and ponder these issues for most of the hike.

Up, up, up. All switchbacks for the next three hours, and whenever I looked back, I still saw the Columbia Gorge. I wondered if I'd ever get out of this basin and onto a flatter trail. I remembered reading that the average hiker could take up to three days to finally hike completely out of the Gorge. So I was only in the first part of Day Two. And with The Rock strapped on my back, I think I was probably below average. It might take me the rest of the summer! And there I went again, judging and comparing myself to some mysterious other.

At about 5:00 p.m. I found a wide spot along the trail and plunked down my pack and sat on the ground with my legs spread out over the cool dirt. I felt like I could simply lie back on my pack and fall asleep until the next day, except for gnawing hunger and no place to pitch my tent or cook a meal. So I decided to sit for a while, drink a couple cups of water, ponder my options, take a quick look at my map, and gather enough energy to press on for a couple more hours or until I found a reasonable camping area. The guidebook and maps didn't show anything close, but these resources were not always accurate. After I'd rested for about ten minutes, along came the first person I had seen since Carla left.

A tall, strapping young man from Washington D.C., Dan was a thru hiker on his way to complete a twenty-five-mile day. He stopped for a moment, and we exchanged pleasantries. Dan was an undergraduate student at Virginia Tech, the very school where my son Noah would be beginning the masters program in civil engineering in the fall. Dan and I exchanged information, and I made a note in my journal to remind me to tell Noah when I returned home. As it turned out, he and Dan did meet later at Virginia Tech and backpacked together along parts of the Appalachian Trail.

After about fifteen minutes of chatting, Dan continued on his way, and I screwed up the energy to hoist The Rock back on and forge ahead. In about another hour, I quite unexpectedly came upon a campsite ten feet off the trail. Though my map didn't indicate there were any campsites in this area, it was perfect, and the last camper had left a stack of firewood with kindling. This is what PCTers call "Trail Magic." And if a person hikes long enough on the PCT, they will experience this "magic" when least expected. The experience usually brings wide grins, sighs of relief, and nods towards the heavens. Trail Magic is just being open to what is in front of us, willing to look at all the possibilities and opportunities gratefully as if they have been a day's gift to us. Perhaps that is why some people never experience it and others do. Over the next several weeks, I experienced Trail Magic in many ways. And I grinned and sighed in gratitude for them each and every time.

I lit a small fire, boiled water for tea, wrote a few thoughts in my journal, took off my boots, leaned back on a rock that was close to the fire, and considered the blessings of the day. I hung my sweaty socks next to the fire and watched their moisture steam. Trail Magic had made it a very good day.

2

DON'T PEE ON THE FOLIAGE

On Day Three I had an unobstructed view of Mt. Hood in the distance and the Gorge was still in sight. It was taunting me. But it was another beautiful morning, and I had slept fairly well after sitting by the campfire, smoking a cigar, and watching the embers die down long into the night. It brought to mind my first backpack trips as a young boy around twelve or thirteen.

It was in the California High Sierras. I was with a small group of other boys around my age, and we were led by Glenn Allen and Don Zerwer, both YMCA directors. I thought about how I owed them for early lessons they taught us about being in the wilderness: respect, etiquette, safety, the use of equipment, building and tending a fire, discerning and choosing safe trails, using common sense, and building self-confidence. That first backpack was a critical experience for me, and it was also the summer I met Bob Jenks, who became my pal, my confidant, and best friend until his death fifty years later. It was also the beginning of a life-long friendship with Glenn that lasted until his death in 2009. I miss them terribly. Don is retired and lives in Arizona.

Even as I write this almost sixty years after that first backpack, I still cringe. Every mistake a young, arrogant, willful boy could make in the out-of-doors I definitely made. But Glenn and Don were never too far off and kept us all from harm's way.

It was Don who told us boys that peeing on the foliage was a basic "no-no" in the wilderness. The salt residue on the leaves left from urine draws attention to the deer and other critters that welcome salt in their diet. To this very day, I do not piss on the foliage. Thus, when I happened upon a hiker one afternoon about two weeks into my PCT hike whom I witnessed peeing on the plush but scarce foliage at his feet, I shared my own earlier wilderness lesson and its rationale. My thoughtful and wise counsel was not met by an open mind. In retrospect, I considered myself fortunate he didn't pee on my boots.

That was my earliest and clearest awareness that there were hikers on the PCT who came with little or no experience and had not learned or been taught the lessons of the wilderness. Nevertheless, I remained persistent and carried my message to whomever I encountered who felt inclined to water the plants.

Journal Entry:
In my tent much later than I had planned, but I hope to sleep more soundly than last night. My old body has to adjust to the hard, cold ground if I'm going to survive this trek. I will simply will myself to adjust.

***

On Day Four, around mid-morning, I reached the crest at 3,400 feet and yelled out a loud farewell to the Columbia Gorge 3,220 feet below and the endless switchbacks up from it. I looked back towards Mt. Hood with a deep sigh of relief that I had a few less taxing miles ahead of me. There is something profoundly discouraging about hiking a long switchback, hiking upwards for hours and never seeming to reach the goal. One corner follows another and the mileage just doesn't feel as though it's adding up. The books are correct; it takes the average hiker nearly three days to climb out of the Gorge.

This was the first day I was somewhat unsettled about the availability of water. I had about eight ounces left, and there was nothing in my guidebook that indicated a water source for several miles.

Water sources are a constant concern for hikers along certain sections of the PCT, because what may be indicated as a water source one year may not be there the next. Weather and snowmelts change from year to year, so nothing about water can ever be taken for granted. Early on, I committed to stopping, hydrating, and filling my water bottles whenever I came upon a water source. Even if I wasn't particularly thirsty, I still stopped and drank as much water as I could stand. There are times when water becomes more important than food. And I learned, as well, there is a vast difference between being thirsty, or my mouth being dry, and my body needing water. A dry mouth doesn't necessarily get a slug of water. "Man up!" I would bark to myself.

3

ONE LOST THING

Somewhere along the trail on the third day of hiking, I lost my trusty, well-worn, red hiking cap. I figured that it had slipped out from where I had tucked it into a side pocket. Maybe it got snagged on a protruding branch. Most likely I simply did a lousy job of securing it, but I wasn't going to retrace a day of hiking for a hat. I'd bought it on sale at REI and worn it for the past several years on various day hikes and backpacks. It had earned the status of a talisman among my collection of hiking gear. Most seasoned backpackers have at least one such item, and mine was a well-worn, red cap.

What made this loss even bitterer was that I so rarely lose things, and when I do, I tend to experience an inordinate amount of self-reproach. Whether a cheap pen or an old, faded handkerchief, I usually feel a strong wave of loss and discontent push against me. I am immediately out of sorts. It's a curious reaction I have known about myself since early childhood. And here's the rub: I know its genesis. But even with that knowledge, I experience little relief. Therapy has been of no use in this matter. Thus, I try not to lose things. And, for the most part, I have been successful. But I missed my red cap.

***

When I was a young boy, around seven or eight, my mother sent me and my older brother, Gaylord, to a military academy within a couple-hour drive from home. I believe she did this from her belief that her two young sons would be better served in an all-male, strict, disciplined environment than in a home headed by a working, overwhelmed, single-parent mother in her early twenties.

As my mother told the story, my birth father returned from the War in the Pacific and rather quickly figured that life with a wife and two toddler sons didn't have the same allure as a bottle of bourbon shared with other women. So one afternoon while my father was out drinking and philandering (I was around three and my brother was five), my gutsy, redheaded, green-eyed, Irish mother packed his belongings and tossed them out on the front lawn. Moreover, she discarded every picture of him. I have no memory of ever seeing him again. From my earliest years, I knew my mother didn't suffer fools.

My father's absence in my young years felt as if someone had dug a big hole in the backyard to plant an enormous tree, then for no apparent reason dropped the shovel and left the yard, leaving that empty, gaping hole behind. I was too young to know anything about the other women or the booze. I was too naïve to understand the relevant relationship between his behavior and a failed marriage. And when I badgered my mother unceasingly— "What happened to Daddy? When's he coming home?"— she simply shrugged a shoulder and looked away. One day I stopped asking. In time, I concocted this convoluted lie that rescued me from the queries of my classmates and brought me some level of status. I was too young to understand how porous and transparent the lie was; I only knew it would rescue me from the moment's humiliation if anyone knew about my alcoholic father who abandoned our family.

My dad was a Navy pilot and was shot down over Tibet on one of his many bombing missions.

There it was. One sentence. One breath. Barely ten seconds of looking into someone's face and telling a fabrication as thin as tissue paper. But what other kid of six or seven years would ever question my deception? Hell, in those days, all our fathers had returned from the War, where all sorts of craziness occurred. But they came home. Home to work. Home to raise their kids. Home to play ball and go camping and barbeque on the back porch. Home to repair broken bicycles and leaky sinks. Home to repair their own brokenness. But my father wasn't home. *My father was a Navy pilot and was shot down over Tibet in one of his many bombing missions.* And presto, I was off the hook. My father was a goddamned war hero. He was God. And if the lie got told long enough to enough people, it would be believed. The truth of it was not the issue. It was what the story did for my young self-preservation. I recreated my own father. I resurrected his pitifully minimal life, and I was saved from the shame of other kids knowing my father was a drunken loser. I was saved from their mean scorn and gossip. I was saved by the power of THE GREAT LIE. And to add to the irony of it all, my mother never knew.

But I remember the very day THE GREAT LIE came to an abrupt end. I was halfway through my senior year in high school. My stepfather had been dead for about two months. A few of my buddies and I were sitting around a table in someone's kitchen and we were talking about biological fathers and stepfathers and who had the most influence. Someone asked what happened to my birth father, and so I told THE GREAT LIE right there in the presence of several buddies. By now I had told the lie for the past dozen years and I had it down pat. I was an actor on stage and recited my well-practiced performance. Then one of the guys interrupted me as I was elaborating on the details and in a very calm and knowing voice simply stated, "But, Glenn, the U.S. never bombed Tibet during any war."

It wasn't an aggressive statement or even a challenge. But right then, I knew the charade was over. I was sick to my stomach as I thought to myself, how the fuck does a high school kid know enough about history to even challenge me? But to my credit, I think I recovered pretty quickly, saying something to the effect that it was what my mother had told me when I was little and I probably got all the facts screwed up. In fact, the story my mother did tell me was that my father was too drunk to be allowed within fifty feet of a bomber and spent his years in the Navy swabbing decks, playing poker, and waiting with abated breath for shore leave when he could go into town to drink and screw. In short, my biological father was a king-sized loser, and the family had hit the Lotto when my stepfather came into our lives.

William Albert Jolley was the kindest and most decent man Mom had ever met, and my brother and I were better off for his being in our lives for the years he was alive. And *that* was the truth.

But until my stepfather did enter our lives, my brother and I were at Page Military Academy, and thus, my earliest male influences were mostly men who had served in some capacity in the Second World War or just back from the Korean Conflict. They were the men who ran the place either as teachers or administrators. This was when I first remembered the terror of a loss.

As a youngster at this institution, I was forever losing my stuff: books, pencils, socks, hats, and just about anything else that wasn't tied down. And whenever I did so, I was punished with a strap across my rear end. These veterans had no patience for a little boy who could manage to lose his own head if it weren't attached to his shoulders. There were times when I wouldn't get the strap to my backside, but was sent to the dormitory and required to sit on my bed, alone, sometimes missing a meal or the evening snacks before bedtime. I do remember a time when I was crying so inconsolably that someone was sent to fetch my older brother (two years my senior) to sit by my side on my bed until I had calmed. I remember on that particular evening he brought graham crackers and shared them, only if I promised to stop my bawling. I must have stopped because I remember eating a whole lot of crackers that night and getting in trouble the next morning for all the crumbs in my bed. My brother brought hope and comfort to me that night. Sometimes I wish he were still alive so I could tell him I remember that simple act of kindness, and thank him.

To this day, I cannot be at peace with the misplacement or loss of things. The psychiatrists are correct when they claim we have substantive understanding about barely ten percent of what we do. But screw all that. I needed my red cap to keep the sun off my balding head.

4

REBELLION ON THE TRAIL

In addition to losing my red cap, the fourth day was the day of my first trail rebellion: I ignored the warning signs posted by an official government agency.

The DNR had posted a sign by the trail that the bridge at Rock Creek was not passable and hikers needed to take an alternate route. The instructions were sketchy and looked to add another two or three miles to an already grueling day. So rather than trusting government directions and adding extra miles, I chose to continue down a steep trail that led to the bottom of a gully. It was about a two-mile hike to the creek. I was the only person in the area and quickly found a perfect campsite just a few feet from the creek's edge.

My first and natural inclination was to look around to see if I was being watched or caught on some hidden camera that would report I had defied the warning sign and needed to be hauled away from my bucolic campsite to appear before the local magistrate. But to my great relief, no repercussions came of my law-breaking decision, and I proceeded to set up camp, take a quick and very cold bath in the stream, collect some wood for a small campfire, make some dinner, and eventually climb into my tent and crawl into the sleeping bag. It was another day of perfect weather, peaceful hiking, and beautiful surroundings. And once again, I hiked the entire day without seeing another hiker. I was quickly becoming at peace with being alone and relishing minimal interaction with others.

The next morning I awoke with anticipation that there truly might be a problem crossing this deep, loud, rushing creek and that the government might have been correct in giving fair warning that the bridge at Rock Creek was, indeed, not passable. So I hurried through another breakfast of instant oatmeal, instant coffee, and a breakfast bar, anticipating the possibility that I would have to hike back out of the gully for the two miles to where the detour began.

Thus far, one of the great thrills of this hike had been experiencing some of the unknowns. I mean, what if the bridge really wasn't passable and what if I had to find a way to get across this rushing body of water and what if...? Last night I had slept within ten feet of the creek, listening to its roaring movement in the still of the peaceful forest, and I surmised that this boisterous creek would not be something I would be able to easily skip across with The Rock on my back. The anticipation of the challenge was both frightening and exhilarating. And I thought about all those early pioneers who crossed hundreds of streams and creeks and rivers on their various journeys across the country to find a better life, and wondered how many times they, too, had some sense of dread that a body of water would not be passable. Perhaps I was a bit dramatic in the comparison, but there was that sense of trepidation about what lay ahead.

Most everything in my life is, to some degree, predictable and settled. I know that the roads back home will be drivable and that the stoplights will work properly, the faucet in the kitchen will work and fill my glass with clean, clear water, the lights will almost without fail turn on with the flick of a switch, and so on and so on. But in the wilderness, there is very little that is definite.

I sat on a log, there in my cozy campsite with the last half of my morning coffee, assuming that the trail was marked and passable and that the bridge really wasn't broken and that I would be able to get to the other side of the stream. So I proceeded with that faith. But I knew there was nothing absolute about any of it. I would just start and, much like life, might have to flail around for a while, take two steps forward and one back, but I knew I would eventually stay the course.

I tossed out the remainder of the coffee, stuck the cup in one of the side pockets of my pack, strapped The Rock on my back, and got back on the trail that led towards the bridge. And behold, within a fourth of a mile there was the bridge, a bit tattered and worse for wear, but quite passable. I smiled at my good fortune so early in the day. I would, after all, get to the other side of Rock Creek. I wouldn't recommend a team of horses pulling a Conestoga wagon across that bridge, but for a hiker weighing in at less than eight hundred pounds, it was as solid as needed. Thus all my trepidations about how to proceed were of no account. In fact, I stood at the middle of the bridge, jumped up and down, yelled up the gorge at the DNR and their false warning, and proceeded up the trail to begin another day of hiking and self-reliance. It was the beginning of Day Five.

5

RESCUED BY TRAIL MAGIC

The goal for Day Five was to camp at Cedar Creek, where, according to the map, there were water and campsites. Yet somehow I managed to miss the spur trail that led the fifty yards off to the creek-side camp. I didn't want to backtrack in search of the trail, so I continued on, hoping to find an alternative site—or at least a water source—as soon as possible. I was down to only ten ounces of water with a dinner to prepare and breakfast the following morning. I had already hiked nearly ten hours, and darkness was closing in by each quarter mile. I felt mild panic creep into my gut.

When it was full-on dark, I rifled through my pack and got out my headlamp and flashlight. I kept hiking with the hope of finding any spot that looked remotely available. Still nothing came into view. I hadn't eaten since around noon, where I had stopped at Panther Creek Campground nearly seven hours earlier. Now I was absolutely exhausted and thirsty, and the trail was getting increasingly more difficult to follow. With every few yards, I felt more and more desperate. Fortunately, there was a full moon. I could go on a bit longer without fear of complete darkness. I hiked at least another three miles until I felt my body was about to give in from pure exhaustion and hunger. I was almost prepared to collapse right there in the middle of the trail with clothes on and no dinner. Just stop, pull out my sleeping bag, and sleep. But quite suddenly and unexpectedly, something very strange and wonderful occurred.

Even with a full moon, a headlamp, and flashlight, I had lost the trail. I looked a few feet all around where I stood and couldn't see any trace that anyone else had walked here. It was as if the trail had ended right where I stood. So I remained still for a long minute until, to my amazement, I noticed a very narrow spur trail to my left where moments before I had seen nothing. I turned towards it, feeling as if something or someone were pulling me forward, as if God were tugging on my sweaty sleeve and directing me to a place to bed for the night. Within five feet I came onto an expansive mesa lit by moonlight, revealing a campsite complete with a rock fire circle, an ample stack of wood, and kindling beside it. I dropped The Rock where I stood and cried out of relief and pure exhaustion. I was awed by my good fortune

Again, "Trail Magic." From what might have been a pure disaster of my own making came a remarkable moment of rescue. And this is where I sat the next morning after a grateful and peaceful night of sleep. But I still needed to find a source of water sooner than not.

**

On the morning of Day Six, I sat by the campfire looking straight ahead at Mt. Adams: massive, snow-covered, and majestic. Its presence dominated the entire northern horizon, and I sipped my cup of lousy coffee, still dazzled by what had occurred the night before.

It was around 7:30 a.m. and I knew I could be on the trail within minutes, but I sat transfixed at the stunning view of the mountain. It was as if I could reach out and touch the snow that clung to its slopes. I also sat retracing the day before and what had gone so abysmally wrong to bring me to a place of near danger and exhaustion. I thought about something I had recently read in one of Frederick Buechner's works, about paying attention to all the moments of our lives, that all moments are key moments.

I've been hiking most my life and I rarely make such critical mistakes. I've embraced the unequivocal truth about backpacking that the devil is in the details. Hiking buddies of mine know me to be cautious to a fault. But speaking for my own defense, all those previous years of the typical five-to eight-day backpack trips were no harbinger to what was in store for me on the PCT; one barely translated into the other.

Forgetting an extra pair of bootlaces on a five-day backpack is inconvenient. On a hundred-mile section of the PCT, such a lapse could prove disastrous. Misgauging the amount of cooking fuel on a long weekend backpack can be overcome by cooking meals on open fires or simply eating one's way through all the dry foods usually meant for energy snacks. Lack of fuel eighty miles before collecting the next reload box could mean disaster. A lost pair of gloves can be remedied by enlisting the extra pair of wool socks. But missing signs for a water source is critical in any hiking experience. And in this particular section, water was especially scarce, so I had come up against a fine line between poor judgment and danger. Within those first days, I knew I could not be sloppy. This was a totally new and uncharted category of backpacking, and it would take more than my Irish resolve and grit. Added to my other newly decreed mantras was yet another: Respect the wilderness. Take nothing for granted. Translated to mean: I must be certain where the water sources are, and if I can't determine from my own maps, I must ask whoever comes along. And yes, be humble. No one succeeds along the PCT without help from someone, sometime.

With about as much self-recrimination as I could tolerate for one day, I packed up and got back on the trail. I walked around the campsite area and gathered up a fairly substantial pile of wood for the next hiker and did the best I could to leave the site looking neat and tidy. On this hike and every hike I had ever experienced, it was always my goal to leave a campsite better than I had found it. It was a lesson I learned as a teenager when hiking with Glenn Allen. "Always leave wood for the next guy, pick up and put in your pocket everything that isn't natural, and leave no trace," would be what Glenn would tell us almost every morning we broke camp. At that time it seemed a bit of overkill and certainly a grand nuisance, but now, looking back on those experiences, he taught us well. Glenn would be pleased that his lessons of campsite maintenance live on.

As I walked away from the campsite, ready to begin the day's hike, I saw that the trail I thought I had lost the night before was right there at my feet, only a few yards away from where I had stopped. In the full light of morning I could see that I was at the juncture of the PCT and Trail 146 and had overshot Cedar Creek by several miles. I shook my head, still dismayed how the day ended with me being guided to a safe place to camp. But at that moment, my concern was for finding water. I was down to about two gulps, and already it seemed that the day was going to be a very hot one.

6

PACKING LIGHTER AND OTHER LESSONS

About five miles into the day, I met a young couple from Wyoming: Steven and Kristen. He was a stud, and she looked as though she'd just stepped out of a fashion magazine. They were hiking from north to south and had come from where I was headed. So, naturally, the first thing I asked was when and where I would come across a water source as I headed north. A mile previously, I'd taken my last swallow of water and was certain they could detect the desperation in my question. They assured me I was one or two miles from a small rill seeping out of the side of the hill. I would pass it on my left.

Then Steve looked down at my pack that was sitting at my feet and with unmasked astonishment blurted, "What the hell is all that shit you're carrying?" And with that, he launched into a mild diatribe about all stuff I should throw out and how if he had the time he would do it for me. He also blasted the thought of ever buying anything more at REI. He was resolute that REI didn't cater to serious long-distance hikers. He had a point, but unfortunately, since there were no other such stores along the trail, I'd just have to make do with the equipment I had already brought. He did leave me with good advice: Unload my pack at my next reload place and send home absolutely everything that was not totally necessary. He believed I could rid myself of about fifteen pounds. They each carried less than twenty pounds and hiked about thirty miles a day.

I told them if I were thirty years old and carrying twenty pounds, I could hike thirty miles a day also, but at seventy I was thankful I was even on the Trail. They were astonished at my age, thinking I was twenty years younger. I liked those people!

Steve was correct. Just over a mile up the trail, I did come across a rill trickling out the side of the hill. The ice-cold water seeping over green, mossy rocks caused a "brain freeze" as I drank with too much haste and desperation. I sat on a rock next to the water source like a troll guarding a bridge and drank for about a half hour until my stomach nearly popped. I filled my water bottles and set off, revived and happy. I swore that would be the last time I would get myself into such a pickle over the lack of water.

***

It was Day Seven and I had been on the Trail for an entire week. I allowed myself a quick moment of self-congratulation. I sat a few feet off the trail with a steep cliff just at my feet as I looked out toward Mt. Adams. From where I rested, I looked downward several hundred feet into a deep and rocky canyon. I could hear the roar of a river coming from its bottom, and I remembered another experience from backpacking in the High Sierras with a group from the local YMCA.

In the summer of 1956 in the High Sierras, twelve of us teenage boys were led by Glenn Allen. One morning, a few of us rose early, collected some food for the day's lunch, grabbed our fishing poles, and lit out towards the lake where we believed we'd catch our limits. After a couple hours of fishing with no luck, we got bored and started looking for some other activity that might satisfy the adventurous spirit of teenage boys. We soon spotted a nearby trail that led to the side of a grand mountain butted up to the meadow where we had been fishing. Up we hiked. It was a very steep trail, but after a couple hours, we were treated to a glorious, panoramic view of the meadow and streams and lakes in the valley below. Now, to any reasonable person, this sight would be sufficient enough to call all our efforts successful. But being the boys we were, each of us took turns to see who could spit the farthest down the side of the mountain and score the longest distant spit. I remember a certain glee in the air as we all took our turns until we simply failed to gather enough saliva in our mouths to spit at all.

And then, out of nowhere, Glenn appeared. He was quietly standing on the trail just a few yards from where we all stood, watching us with his signature intensity that silently informed us we had crossed some invisible line of decency or, worse, broken some ancient, primordial rule about the wilderness. We all ceased the spitting and, without a word of direction, silently made our way down the mountain trail to our campsite. No fish were caught that day and nothing was said about the spitting incident until that night after dinner around the campfire. Songs were sung and we bragged about who had the biggest fish hit their lines and get away and who had the *cojones* to finally jump into the frigid, alpine lake where we were camped. Then there was a pregnant pause as we boys looked into the crackling embers of the campfire. Glenn cleared his throat and begun to speak in his usual slow, measured, and economical fashion.

"Boys," he began, "up here we have the great privilege to be in the presence of what the Almighty has created and that we are required to be good stewards of." And then he paused, took a deep breath, and continued to look into the fading embers as if there were words written on them that he was seeking to decipher. "You never spit into the work of God."

And that was all he said. But we knew what he meant. Now, understand, at that age, I hadn't fashioned a very well-developed worldview that could make any sense of the right or wrong about spitting down a cliff into a valley. I think we were more concerned about disappointing Glenn than offending the Almighty and committing some egregious sin against Creation. I think, too, he was giving his best shot to inform us that we had to earn the right to be in the wilderness. These were among my earliest lessons burnt into my consciousness. They still inform me there are certain ways to comport oneself in the wilderness and beyond.

To this day, whenever I am tempted to spit down a cliff, I remember that night around the campfire staring into the embers while Glenn spoke. His legacy and lessons he taught about the wilderness remain deep in my being. I think, at this juncture of my life, Glenn would concur that I've earned the right to be on the PCT.

***

Back on the trail in the Indian Heaven Wilderness, I met three young Buddhist monks walking from the town of Trout Lake, where they shared a house. They were on a short pilgrimage to a monastery in central Oregon, where they planned to join fellow monks for their annual sharing of prayers and meditation. Despite all the sacrifices that such a life must entail, it seemed like a very fine way to spend one's energy and life. They were robed in typical Buddhist garb, wearing sandals rather than hiking boots, and each had a staff made from local wood. After a half hour of chatting, we all went our separate ways with hugs and well wishes. It was an unexpected and wonderful interlude to the day. It wasn't until several minutes later that I realized none of the monks were carrying much of a pack for such a long journey. It seemed as though each were carrying a daypack with hardly enough room for the amount of equipment it would require before reaching their destination.

I figured I would have to hike twenty miles this day and the next to arrive in Trout Lake, where my first reload box was waiting. Again, if I were a twenty-two-year-old, I could do it, but given the elevation changes, the switchbacks, the general terrain, and the assorted blisters on both feet, it would be a stretch.

Around noon I came to the sign that pointed towards Blue Lake, a fourth mile off the trail. The lake is nestled at the foot of Gifford Peak and invites the hiker to sit and stay awhile. Had I arrived later in the day, it would have been a natural place to camp for the night. But it was around noon and time to break for lunch. Now, when most people think of lunch, what usually comes to mind are sandwiches in some form, salads of various ingredients, soups, etc. My lunches were quick and simple and usually consisted of trail mix (nuts, M&Ms, dried fruits), some kind of protein bar, a candy bar, and lots of water. Only on rare occasions would I take the time and energy to unpack my stove and cook a hot lunch. Usually some of each of those items would sufficiently fill me up. Eating too much usually left me wanting to take a nap, which I rarely took time to do.

As I approached what appeared to be a perfect spot to stop, I saw a man fishing and a small donkey standing close by tethered to a tree. As I came closer, I noticed the man was wearing a handgun on his hip. Oh shit, I thought. Could this be one of those folks who roam the mountains with their donkeys killing off us infidels who dare invade their space? Well, no, it was none of that. And the tethered beast was not a donkey but rather a miniature mule named Rowdy that his owner, JR, had rescued from the kill block several years prior. Rowdy accompanied JR whenever he went into the mountains to fish or hunt. We sat by the lake while JR fished and I ate my simple dry lunch. After a few minutes of chatting around several subjects, I broached the question about the holstered pistol strapped to his hip.

"Well, what you think I'm gonna do if ol' Rowdy here falls and breaks a leg? You think I'm gonna drag his smelly ass off this mountain? Hell no, I'm gonna shoot him and kick him over a cliff and let nature take care of the rest."

I nodded as if to assure him that was the very best answer any sane and sensitive human being could offer up.

But then JR went on, "And too, once in a while I come across these folks with dogs that want to take a run at ol' Rowdy here. And if they ever got too close and I thought they'd hurt my mule, hell, I'd just shoot the little shits and let the owners take care of the rest."

Again, I nodded as if in total agreement with how JR would solve the problem of menacing canines. All the time JR was looking out on the lake, waiting for a fish to take the bait. No luck. I had a thought they may have looked up and seen the gun on his hip and decided to swim away.

I finished my lunch and packed up to start again. JR took a couple of pictures of me and I took one of Rowdy. Another fascinating encounter along the Trail.

Seeing JR packing a sidearm and a rifle sheathed and strapped to the side of his mule brought to mind some of the conversations I had had with folks back home about guns and whether or not I would carry one on the PCT.

"You taking a gun with you?" I was often asked.

"Why?"

"Well, for protection?"

"Protection from what?"

"Bears, snakes…maybe there's a few crazies out there."

"Um, I think I'd be more apt to run into crazies at a mall than in the wilderness."

I would explain that where I was going there were no poisonous snakes and the black bears that inhabited the Cascades were rarely a threat to anyone's safety. It was in the California Sierras where the bears were more troublesome and were known to raid campsites, tear into cars, and create general havoc for anyone carrying food or the smell of food.

Nevertheless, there were ample folks who believed that having a gun would make me safer while alone in the wilderness. But I would explain that, to my knowledge, there wasn't a handgun powerful enough to drop an eight-hundred-pound bear lunging towards me at thirty miles an hour. And if there were such a weapon, there exists the false assumption I would be capable of maintaining a calm and steady resolve long enough to load the thing with bullets I'd packed away in some side pocket of my pack and get off at least one shot before feeling the first painful strike of claws tearing away my face or razor-sharp teeth burying deeply into my throat.

As for snakes, well, I doubt anyone other than Annie Oakley could shoot and hit the slithering rascal. And forget about a mountain lion lunging onto my backside from a nearby tree branch before I could even turn my head around to scream out one final, "Oh Shit!"

As for the "bad people" I might encounter, "Ask yourself this question: Why would anyone hike for days in the mountains to accost an old man whose only valuables are trail mix, a pocket knife, and dirty socks?" I am at more risk walking from my parked car at a shopping mall than I am in the wilderness. And that same sense of safety also applies to all the women I encountered along the Trail. The women I met, hiking solo or with a friend, didn't express any concerns about safety or fear of strangers. If asked about their concerns about safety, their response was something in the order of being more fearful of walking to their car after an evening of shopping at a mall than hiking in the wilderness areas. Simply stated, during both summers on the PCT, there was never a moment when I felt at risk or sensed danger from another human being. Annoyed? Yes. Fearful? No.

And too, the gospel of all serious backpackers is to hike with as light a pack as possible. The extra pounds of a handgun and bullets would be unnecessary weight.

I get it. We live in fearful times. Nevertheless, despite all the messages of warnings and suggestions to pack a weapon, I chose confidence over fear, I chose self-assurance over self-doubt, and I chose to trust my past experiences and successes over misgivings or past failures. In the end, I chose to trust God. Guns on the PCT? I think not.

7

NAKED IN THE LAKE

It was around three in the afternoon and the day had been one of the hottest yet. I came to several water sources during the day and followed my rule of hydrating and filling my water bottles whenever I came to a water source. I wasn't taking any more chances. I could see a small lake to my left about fifty yards off the trail, down a steep slope. According to my map, it was Bear Lake, about sixty miles from where I'd begun several days before, and I decided this would be the day to experience my first skinny-dip along the PCT.

I dropped The Rock by the trail and headed towards the lake. Seeing no other hikers or campers in view, I stripped, left my clothes in a pile on the shore, and jumped into the cold, clear, inviting water, splashing around in pure joy. My God, I couldn't remember when I had experienced anything as wonderful as that naked swim in that remote lake on that hot day in the summer of 2012.

How many more opportunities in my life would I have to jump into a mountain lake, buck-naked? I would never again be at this specific place in this particular lake, so I reveled in those moments of cool, cold refreshment. If I lost an hour of hiking and had to put my dry clothes back on my half-dried body, so what? It was worth every minute. I was not committed rigidly to any schedule, and there was no one waiting for me to arrive anywhere at any specific time. Though having only two days of food left, I needed to be in Trout Lake soon. So I got dressed, headed the fifty yards up the slope, strapped on The Rock, and hiked north again. I felt clean and revived. I couldn't remember the last time I'd swum naked in a lake. Was it in my youth with the YMCA or with some buddies as an adult backpacking in the Washington Cascades? Whenever it was, it had been too long. Those exhilarating few moments will stay with me always.

About two hours past Bear Lake, with the evening coming upon me and knowing I would not make the twenty-mile goal I had hoped for that morning, I stopped along the path to look at one of my maps for a place to camp in the next four to six miles. A young couple out for a short backpack came down the trail. Both were in their late twenties and obviously in their mutually attentive early stage of love. She was an avid camper and he had never slept in a tent or hiked a distance more than a few blocks to the local Starbucks for a twelve-ounce double latté. For whatever reason, they felt compelled to share that they were in the first few weeks of their newfound relationship. I told them camping with someone was a great way to get to know that person, if perhaps a bit risky. She agreed, but he seemed a little baffled by my comment. They asked if I knew of a place nearby where they could camp with some privacy and where there was water. I told them about Bear Lake just down the trail about two hours. They were thrilled at the prospect. I envied them both. We said our farewells, and they headed towards Bear Lake. Suddenly I felt a pang of loneliness for the first time since I had left Carla by the side at the Columbia Gorge. It was one of a number of times I wished she had joined me.

Carla is not a backpacker. Oh, she does enjoy a challenging day hike, but at the end of the day, she wants a hot meal, a glass of wine, a shower, and a comfortable bed. The idea of carrying a heavy pack, sleeping on cold, unforgiving ground, and going days without washing her hair is simply unappealing. Why anyone would choose to be so uncomfortable and cold and grimy is beyond her imagination. Why do I do it? The best answer I can conjure is simply, "Because I enjoy it."

As I stood watching the couple head down the trail towards the lake, I was still thinking about Carla and wondered what it would be like to share all this with her, the same beauty, the same air, the wonder, the lakes, the sunsets, the peace that ends a perfect day, an intimacy we will never have. And that thought saddened me. I wondered if the days of our exploring a deeper intimacy were over. In those moments, it felt as though they were, and that thought saddened me even further. But my sadness was mixed with gratitude. I knew that, without Carla, I could not be on the Trail. It was not merely that she had lent so much support in all the preparations and was my "fall back" person if anything went awry. No, Carla actually saved my life. I was drowning, slipping deeper and deeper into self-destruction. And her presence and love dragged me kicking and screaming back into life.

But now, I wanted more and didn't even know what that might look like or how to even frame a request. "Let it go," I told myself, "and be grateful for what is." And yet, intimacy might be the last frontier in our lives together. Notwithstanding that insight, I had an unshakable awareness that when I married Carla, I'd hit the lottery and regrettably spent many years squandering that abundant treasure. With her, and others, I was stumbling along on a long road towards redemption.

***

It was about 8:00 p.m. and the day had been a full one: thoughts about lessons from Glenn, the meeting of monks, the encounter with JR and his mule Rowdy, a buck-naked swim in the lake, the encounter with the young-in-lust couple. I was ready to stop even though I hadn't made my mileage goal—again! I thought that maybe, for the sake of my own sanity, I should just give up the whole goal thing and simply hike the day, stop along the way as I pleased, and sometime around six to seven start looking for a campsite with water. Otherwise, I thought, I'd just keep setting myself up for failure.

Soon enough, I came across a small, inviting meadow that seemed a natural place to camp for the night. There appeared to be no signs that anyone had camped there in the near past and there was no water source, but I had both my bottles filled so I was in good shape. As I began to pitch my tent, I looked over my shoulder and saw that I had a full-on view of Mt. Adams. In the course of the miles I had hiked that day, I had seen Mt. Rainier, Mt. Hood, and now Mt. Adams. Such beauty right there at my feet, literally! I had about an hour of daylight, so I prepared dinner then put everything else in its place before nightfall. I gathered enough wood for a small fire, took out my last cigar, and settled back to enjoy the view and the last few minutes of a beautiful, sunlit day. Most evenings after dinner, when I sat by the fire, I wrote something in my journal, and I often prayed. It seemed like a good and appropriate ritual to have settled upon.

In the many years that I have camped in the backcountry, I have experienced a lot of day-ending campfires. But at this stage of my life, I was deeply aware there would be fewer, not more, of those perfect days and campfires. Now each was a gift for which I was thankful.

Journal Entry:
I seem to pray more as I get older. Simple prayers are mostly about gratitude. Often for Carla and the children. Sometimes for myself. Prayer seems to come more naturally and easily now. I wonder why it took me so long to understand that each day is a gift and there is wonder in every moment if I simply take the time to look. I think about how my life might have been lived differently had I embraced that simple thought. Not in a pious or sanctimonious way, but in a way that was peaceful and graceful. At the end of the day, my prayer is simply, "Hi, God. Thanks for the day. Goodnight."

I thought about those sorts of things on the long hours of hiking. Not constantly or morbidly, but reflectively. Pondering was a good way to let the hours of each day pass without thinking much how my feet hurt or my back ached or how I could have planned certain things about this hike more efficiently. For all the weeks and months of planning prior to taking my first step, there were still gaps in the final plans for which I was paying the price each day. Nothing huge, but enough so that, had I been a little more attentive, the days would have been easier.

8

THE MANY MANIFESTATIONS OF TRAIL ANGELS

By Day Eight I was about twenty miles from Trout Lake, a small mountain village from where a person can view the magnificent Mt. Adams. I awoke around five in the morning. It was still pitch dark, so I lingered in my warm sleeping bag for another hour before rising and boiling a pot of water for coffee and instant oatmeal. Eight days into the hike and already sick of instant oatmeal. I would force it down knowing that oatmeal was a quick source of energy and an easy meal to prepare. I can't hike on an empty stomach. I just wished I had some half and half, brown sugar, and a fresh banana to slice atop the bowl. I finished up breakfast, such as it was, packed up the tent, stuffed the sleeping bag into my pack, and headed down the trail towards Road 23, where I dropped my pack. I then headed off to the creek that was running through a state park where several campers were still in their tents and campers. I took a bar of soap and a small towel from my pack so I could enjoy a quick "spit bath" before heading into Trout Lake.

I returned to where The Rock lay, put away the soap, and spread the towel over the pack to dry in the morning sun. I then started to walk up and down the dirt road looking for the trailhead that was supposed to bring me closer to town, but after about an hour of searching, I couldn't find the damned thing. It seemed that it should have been more obvious. So I just sat down by my pack and waited. I had done this a couple of times thus far on the hike. When in doubt, I sat and waited, and usually another PCTer would come along within a short period of time and tell me whether or not I was headed in the right direction. And, as always, I had enough provision in my pack to wait it out for several days, though that never happened.

I held an unshakable and intractable belief that I had not come to the mountains to get lost and that help was always near. What was also as true was knowing that in life, as in hiking, part of the experience is to get comfortable with the fact that one will get lost, and it is just as true that one will also get found. Besides, I had concluded, I was never truly lost, rather, just momentarily in a "circle of confusion."

So I sat at midmorning on the side of a dirt road in a circle of confusion, waiting for clarity, when along came an SUV roaring down that dusty dirt road. It stopped right alongside where I was sitting. I jumped up as the passenger rolled down his window.

A burly, bearded, middle-aged man took a long, hard up-and-down look at me then called out, "You're either lost or crazy or needing a ride or all three, so hop in!" He offered the invitation without even knowing where I was headed or knowing anything about me. I quickly threw my pack and poles into the back seat and jumped in next to my stuff. Off we went towards Trout Lake, leaving clouds of dust in our wake.

Linda and Thomas were a couple from a small town on the border of Oregon and Washington out for a Sunday drive. Within a few minutes of driving, he reached back to where I was sitting next to a cooler, popped open the top, and grabbed a cold can of beer. He offered one to me, and I declined, claiming it was too early for me. He just shrugged his shoulders and proceeded to enjoy his can of brew. And for the next fifteen miles, as we rambled towards town, we chatted about each other's current lives. They were fascinated by the fact someone my age was hiking alone for such a long distance. I was interested in their relationship and their lives together in a small town.

They drove me to the Trout Lake General Store, where I picked up my first reload box from Carla, then drove me to the city park a little north of town, where I chose a campsite from the many that were vacant. We said our goodbyes and off they went. I took out my sleeping pad, found a nice shady spot under a tree, and opened my box. Along with all the necessary items I had packed prior to my leave, Carla had added some special goodies along with a sweet note.

Hope this finds you safe and enjoying your adventure. I miss my friend.

I took off my boots, opened a can of root beer I had purchased at the store, and settled in to relax in the shade. I planned to spend the day and night in Trout Lake and so was in no hurry to set up camp or find the town's only restaurant. About two hours later, still comfortably leaning against a shady tree with my bare feet exposing a host of blisters, I saw a familiar SUV drive through the park looking for me. The car stopped close to where I was sitting. The burly man got out of the car holding the trekking poles I had inadvertently left on the back seat of their car. They had driven for nearly an hour before he saw them sitting there and then drove all the way back to Trout Lake, knowing I most likely wouldn't be able to continue to hike without them. They were right.

He was none too happy as he handed the poles to me with the comment, "So I guess it'll take a full-blooded Indian to get a white guy across the mountains." He shook his head in a mock disgust, and then quipped, "Hell, some things never change!" And off they drove.

They were Trail Angels if ever there were.

9

RELOAD BOXES

The subject of supplies and how a PCT hiker gets them comes up in almost any conversation when asked about my experience. So I think a few words about the matter bear explaining.

The Pacific Crest Trail Association maintains a complete list of places along the Trail, from start to finish, where a package can be sent. Typically these designated places are within a few days to a week of each other. Where a hiker stops and retrieves a package depends on how spry, speedy, and determined he or she is. A healthy, athletic youngster hiking between twenty-five and forty miles per day will require fewer reload packages. For an older hiker, who may walk slower and hike less miles, he will need to carry more supplies and consequently stop more frequently for a reload box. And to add insult to injury, that hiker will typically carry a heavier pack. Seems a bit unfair in the realm of things, but that's one of the harsh realities of the PCT: All is fair in love and hiking. Given my age with a mild case of COPD, several painful blisters, and an aching right foot, I required seven to nine days to cover a hundred miles and carried a pack weighing thirty-eight to forty-two pounds. Younger hikers carried twenty to thirty pounds—seldom more and rarely less.

As I met more and more PCT hikers, both the thru hikers and the sectional ones, I learned variations on how each of us obtained our resupplies. In my case, I'd packed all my supplies before I'd left home. The garage had looked like a small corner grocery store. I calculated that for the five-hundred-plus miles of the Washington section, I would need six resupply boxes, each one with appropriate food amounts, fresh socks, toilet paper, etc. All those items I packed into boxes with instructions to Carla when and where to send them. She sent each box about a week before

I was scheduled to arrive at that specific place. And to my delight, Carla always added some fresh oranges, a bag of my favorite cookies (ginger snaps), a few bars of chocolate, and a very sweet note of encouragement. Opening a new reload box was a reminder of my youth when my mother would sent me a "CARE package" full of all the stuff I wasn't supposed to eat while at camp. By the time I had hiked a week, I already had forgotten what I had packed before my leave, so opening the box was pure glee.

Most places that accepted a reload box did so with great generosity of spirit and would keep them for several weeks beyond the declared date of arrival. And most places put no charge on that service. When I arrived for my first reload box at Trout Lake, the women at the Trout Lake General Store had all the boxes in a designated corner by the front of the store. And, of course, while in the store, we all purchased what we could not pack in our boxes: cold drinks, cheeses, lunchmeats, etc. It was a win/win for us and the stores that kept our packages. And most places also became somewhere a hiker might take a zero day (a day off from hiking), settle in, and rest.

After my Trail Angels left me with my poles, I set up camp for the night, found the pay showers in the park, and spent the remainder of the day loafing around the front porch of the general store, walking around the small town, and eventually walking the hundred yards to the local café that served the very finest huckleberry ice cream, huckleberry milkshakes, and huckleberry pancakes I've ever devoured. This was huckleberry country, and they proudly made the most of it.

***

There was a category of hikers who got their supplies through a method called a "bump-box," which simply means that the box was packed and sent from one particular place to the next by the hiker himself. Thus the hiker who arrived at the store in Trout Lake would have sent himself a package from the Columbia Gorge, and once at White Pass would have sent himself a package from Trout Lake, and on and on throughout the entire PCT. He just "bumped" his packages to himself.

There was another and much smaller group of hikers who didn't choose to deal with reload boxes of any sort. They relied on the generosity of other hikers who left unwanted supplies in what is called "the hiker's box" at each designated stop. As an example, at Trout Lake, I realized I had more instant oatmeal and dehydrated dinners than I either wanted or needed, so I left them in the hiker's box for someone else to take. People left all sorts of things in those boxes: new socks, unwanted trekking poles, foodstuffs of all kinds. And if there weren't enough supplies in the box, those same hikers would supplement their supplies by purchasing items at a local store along the way. They just made it work for them without the expense and hassle of having a reload box sent. I wasn't that courageous or trusting of others' generosity.

While at Trout Lake and taking a zero day, I took the advice of the young couple I had met a few days before: I emptied my pack and sorted out everything I absolutely did not need, packed it up in another box, and sent it home. In so doing, just like they'd said, I lightened my pack by nearly ten pounds!

How can that happen? Simple. I made three piles: The first pile for everything absolutely necessary for the hike (stove and fuel, tent, sleeping bag, toilet paper, a second pair of socks, etc.); the second pile for all the items I thought may be needed but was unsure of (extra flashlight, third pair of socks, extra food, two books to read, etc.); and a third pile that included everything I knew for certain I didn't need (five extra batteries, four pens, two extra pairs of hiking shorts, a large hunting knife, etc.). I packed the first pile in my backpack and sent the other two piles home or left in the hiker's box what I didn't want or need. In truth, I didn't miss anything from the two piles I sent home and certainly didn't miss lugging those extra ten pounds on my back.

The entire matter of pack weight brought to mind all the years I carried a sixty-to-seventy-pound pack and felt miserable for the entire hike. I just believed it came with the territory so sucked it up and kept walking. In my defense, I often had one or more of my children with me, so I was carrying a lot of their stuff. What a grand relief to realize I could carry a pack so much lighter and have what I needed for a safe and comfortable hiking experience. It was the beginning of an ongoing reflection that I had too much stuff in general in my life and needed to think radically of how to live more simply and, yes, lightly.

10

TROUT LAKE

To my knowledge and amusement, there was no actual lake in Trout Lake. So why the name? I couldn't find anyone who knew. Although lacking a lake, the town had other amenities worth commenting upon. "Friendly" is what mostly comes to mind; it was a town full of Trail Angels. They welcomed us into their midst and encouraged us to ask if there was anything they could do to make our stay more comfortable. In fact, the owner of the general store had a couple of rooms in the back of her store she offered to any PCT hiker for $20.00, laundry and showers included. When I retrieved my box, I wasn't aware of this offer and headed straight to the city park, where I made camp for $6.00 and paid another $4.00 for the public showers. I hand-washed my clothes at the faucet at my camp. It all worked, and I practically had the entire camp to myself, so I didn't miss not taking advantage of the rooms. But my point was about their generosity and welcoming spirit.

Unfortunately, a lot of PCT hikers bypass Trout Lake because, once reaching Road 23, it's a fifteen-mile hitchhike to town. About half the hikers I met were headed straight to White Pass, eighty miles north. From the trailhead at Columbia Gorge to White Pass was about 150 miles. For me, that would have meant carrying enough food and supplies to last that stretch of ten to fourteen days. It would be too much weight for me, so I chose to cut the section from the Gorge to White Pass nearly in half. Besides, the day I arrived in town, the temperature was tipping just a bit over 100 degrees. It was a good day to stop and rest.

In the middle of the afternoon on Day Eight, and my first day in Trout Lake, I decided to do a little exploring. I wondered what sort of people lived in such a confined and tiny place. I knew something of this because I live in a small community on an island in Puget Sound, and if you were to ask my children, they would tell you it's like living on a rock. They're all drama queens. But Trout Lake is a community even smaller than my hometown, having only one café, one store, and one gas station a few miles out of town. It looked as though several small businesses had begun and failed. Within a few blocks from where I was camping, I came upon the small, white-clad, A-frame First Presbyterian Church of Trout Lake. The door was unlocked, so I entered, partially to explore and partially to get out of the heat. The sanctuary was musty and dark and looked like so many other small, underused churches of its kind.

It brought to mind a small church where I once served as a visiting preacher when I was a young seminarian. In those days I'd thought I had something to say to hardworking, salt-of-the-earth farmers and ranchers raising crops and animals and children. I walked to the front of the church, turned around, and tried to imagine myself fifty years ago speaking with confidence and brashness. I shuddered to think of what God-awful nonsense I preached on any given Sunday morning. I can only imagine they sat quietly in their pews with considered patience and forbearance, giving the benefit of the doubt to this young fool while silently hoping and praying he would soon come to his senses and learn something about the world before he did more damage.

Before I left, I wrote a short note in the visitor's book on a table near the front of the church, closed the door tightly as I left, and headed towards town, shaking my head, laughing quietly to myself.

11

FARM DOGS AND ANOTHER TRAIL ANGEL

The previous day, around 4:00 p.m., I was in the Trout Lake Post Office, waiting at the counter and preparing to send all the extra supplies back home, when a woman approached me and asked if I had just come off the Trail. I said I had, and she offered to take me back to trailhead whenever I was ready to resume the hike. When I told her I wanted to stay the day and leave after breakfast, she offered to meet me at the local restaurant around 9:00 a.m. Sure enough, the next morning, Linda drove up in her SUV and we began the fifteen-mile drive to the trailhead. It was lovely encounter with an older woman who had recently lost her husband to cancer. They had met in high school and settled in Trout Lake, where they lived for over forty years. Linda had been a Trail Angel for the past twenty years and was proud of all the times she had come to the assistance of PCT hikers. We parted with a hug and blessings. Another example of how the universe provided me with assurances.

With Trout Lake behind me, and with loads of good memories, I headed towards White Pass about sixty-five miles north. And depending on which map I read, I was either (or both) in the Indian Haven Wilderness or the Gifford Pinchot National Forest.

***

On Day Ten, I was on the trail by around 10:00 a.m. Later than I usually started, but the breakfast and sharing time with Linda was worth the late start. The hike was fairly straightforward until mid-afternoon, when I came to the edge of an expansive snowdrift. I'm not very adept at accurately describing the size of a particular area, but I figured it was the size of a football field. It was certainly large enough that I could not see where the trail began again at the other side of the snow. This was a major problem and the first time I questioned if I could continue the hike. I stood at the base of the snowfield and looked ahead to see if I could see any footprints from previous hikers. I couldn't. So, I removed my pack and sat on a rock nearby, considering my options. Do I dare begin walking out on the drift only to discover I had headed in the wrong direction? Do I turn around and head back to Trout Lake and consider other options? Do I wait for another hiker who's willing to let me follow him across the field? With such questions swirling around in my head, I sat and chewed on some trail mix, fully aware I couldn't simply stay sitting on a rock waiting for divine intervention. Or could I?

Months earlier, in the face of all sorts of input and suggestions, I chose not to carry a GPS. First, I am what my children refer to as "technologically challenged," meaning I don't have a clue how to use and take advantage of what has been around for over a decade. I chose the most familiar and least complicated gear. Maps and parts of guidebooks gave me good directions. However, what no map could offer was the condition of the trail at any particular section.

On the other hand, during the course of a day, I met hikers along the trail (mostly my children's ages) who, with their GPS and apps readily in hand, could determine nearly every inch of the trail and whatever challenges lay ahead. And in the case of a snowfield, their GPS would mark a direction for them to follow even with the trail buried several feet in snow. But even at this low point, when I questioned the wisdom of my choice, I still believed I had made the correct one for me. Then and now, I hold fast to my position on the use of a GPS or PCT app. It has to do with wonder and mystery and surprise. I want every day to be surprise. I want to come around a corner or hike up to a saddle and look out towards some distant view and feel a rush of discovery. I want to sit on a log and pore over my maps and figure out where I missed the trail and where to find it again. I don't want to look at a screen and see what a campsite ten miles ahead will look like. I want to arrive at that place and see it for the first time. I know it's both natural and tempting to want to know something about where we're going before we begin. But sometimes the answers are in the doing. What I needed to know was always revealed, and it was usually better than I had imagined.

Absent the technology, I sat on a tree stump with The Rock at my feet and tossed another handful of trail mix into my mouth and waited and looked out at the snowfield that had stubbornly refused to melt by mid-August.

Earlier in the day I had met a middle-aged man with his two enormous dogs who passed me about an hour into the day. With his dogs leading the way, he was headed towards some spur trail to check out a lake, the name of which I forgot the moment he named it. I hadn't given any more thought to that encounter until I heard a racket coming up the trail. I stood up, a bit startled, hoping it wasn't a couple of bear cubs following their momma bear. That could spell disaster. I had barely given myself much time to work up a full anxiety attack when out of the trees came Peter and his two rambunctious dogs! And he was holding a GPS! As they approached, he started laughing and shaking his head. He knew right off what my dilemma was. The dogs didn't stop. They just ran out onto the snowdrift with pure delight and unbounded energy. If I hadn't been so distressed, I would have shared in the laughter.

"Looks like you could use some help," Peter spoke out as he came towards me.

"Pretty obvious, huh?"

"You could say that."

"I *could* use some help," I said, which are words I rarely hear myself saying.

Peter told me he was in no hurry that day and would gladly hold back on his hiking pace and walk me through the snow to wherever the trail began again. I nearly cried at his kindness and my good fortune. Yet another Trail Angel appeared to rescue the day. For the next hour, Peter led with his eyes glued to the GPS and me walking into every impression his boots made in the snow, and we eventually made it across the drift. At the edge of the snowdrift, we parted company, and I watched him head down the trail following his dogs, who seemed to know from the beginning how to make it across the snow without guidance, just their own good instincts.

***

On Day Eleven I awoke to a beautiful, crisp morning. As I hovered over my stove and looked out to the horizon, I could see a clear and unobstructed view of Mt. Rainier. The prior night I had camped in the same site as Peter. Though he went ahead of me after getting through the snowdrift, we eventually met up at the end of the day. Of course, by the time I reached him, he had already pitched his tent, collected some firewood, and eaten dinner. I think we were equally surprised to see one another as I came around the bend towards his camping area. He invited me to share the space. And so I did.

Sharing a campsite was a usual occurrence along the PCT. It's a *mi casa, su casa* mind set. If a person has set up camp and there is room for at least one more sleeping bag, a hiker is most likely welcome to share. That was my own experience on several occasions. There were times I would be sitting around a small campfire at the end of the day when I might see a headlamp in the distance. Within a few minutes I'd hear a voice calling out of the darkness, "Hey, is there room for one more?" "Always room for one more," I'd say. It was just so with Peter and me.

At fifty-two, Peter had recently sold his wheat farm in central Oregon and was finding ways to fill his time. I didn't ask and he didn't offer the details, but I suspect he made enough from the sale that afforded him to take about as much time as he wanted and do about anything he wanted to do. Backpacking was his passion, so this is what he did. That day I was the grateful beneficiary of that choice.

After breakfast, Peter offered to hike with me until we got through the worst of more snowfields to come and on to lower elevations. Though he maintained a much faster pace than me, he was willing to hold back. So for the next several hours we beat a path across several snowfields, across a couple of raging creeks, and finally snowless trails. Satisfied that the worst was behind us, Peter took off at his own pace. With his two large, frisky dogs bounding ahead of him, he was soon out of sight. We had parted with a handshake and well wishes. I told him he was my Trail Angel of the week. He looked down at the ground and kicked up some dirt in seeming embarrassment. Peter was a farmer not used to such expressions of gratitude.

When he left, I dumped The Rock by the trail and ate some lunch. I figured I would not see Peter again and that at any given time during the course of the day he would be at least an hour ahead of me. I had hiked a little over eighteen miles the previous day and was still feeling the effects, so I took more time for lunch than usual. Back-to-back long mileage was challenging for me at this early stage of the PCT, so I allowed myself time to rest and recover whenever it seemed reasonable.

***

The morning of Day Twelve was foggy and cold. I hadn't slept well, even after an eighteen-mile day. You'd think one would fall into bed and pass out from sheer exhaustion. Not so. Most nights I found it very difficult to sleep. I was comfortable and warm, but it seemed my muscles and nerves would simply not relax. I decided that, the next place I could, I would purchase some kind of sleeping aid.

Just as I was thinking of ending the day and looking for a campsite, I saw a small, white piece of paper stuck to the branch of a bush jutting out next to the trail.

Glenn, go right.

I did. Peter had found a large, flat area about fifty feet off the trail and was sitting next to a small campfire on the backpack chair he had brought along, sipping tea. The dogs were at his feet enjoying the warmth. It was a postcard scene.

"Jesus, I can't get rid of you and those ratty dogs!" I said. Actually, I was relieved and delighted to see him.

"Oh, shut up and set yourself up. I'm hungry and been waiting for your sorry ass to catch up. I almost set the dogs loose to find you!"

That evening we sat around the campfire and talked about our lives and marriages and work and some of our past backpacking experiences. Peter was good company, the sort of person I could envision hiking with in the future. But he was a day behind getting to White Pass, where he planned to meet his wife. So for the next two days he would need to cover close to forty miles. There was no way I could maintain that pace, especially given the soreness of my feet and the terrain we were about to encounter. From where we were camped to White Pass along Highway 12, there would be a series of tough switchbacks and then a difficult trudge across the side of a snowy mountain up to Cispus Pass, followed by the Goat Rock Wilderness. All were formidable challenges, especially with a pack that seemed to get heavier, not lighter, by the day. Carla was wrong. No matter how much food I ate, the weight of The Rock seemed to stay constant. There was something amiss about the physics of the whole thing.

12

THE FALL AND OTHER ANGELS

The previous day's hike had been long and arduous. Peter and I leapfrogged one another throughout the passing hours. Either he was slowing down to care for his dogs or I was picking up my pace. We had agreed that at the end of the day he would set up camp along Sheep Lake, about two miles south of Cispus Pass. He offered to hike with me the next morning across the expansive snowfield to assure that I would cross it safely. It was an immensely kind offer, given that he was trying to make as much mileage as possible and I sensed he was getting a bit weary of my company. We had both started the PCT with intentions to hike alone and here we were practically hiking together for the past three days. I think I was benefiting more from his company than he from mine. Nevertheless, he did find a nice area along the lake, and about an hour later I came trudging into the camping area totally beat. My feet hurt like hell, my back ached, I was hungry beyond adjectives, and I wanted a hot shower. But what I settled for was simply reaching a campsite next to Sheep Lake, a place to pitch my tent, a small campfire to warm the high altitude's chilly evening, and a very large helping of a quick-fix Mexican rice dinner, topped off with a busted-up chocolate bar for dessert. And I was still hungry. Had I been more confident in my ability to hike the forty miles to White Pass in a two-day stretch, I would have eaten another one of the three dinners I had packed for this section. Instead, I settled on a couple handfuls of trail mix.

The next morning I took a sort of "screw it" mentality, broke out one of the three remaining dinner packets, and fixed one for breakfast. I couldn't remember when I had eaten beef stew for breakfast, but I couldn't face another serving of instant oatmeal. I knew it would be a hard day of hiking, so the extra calories in the stew would be helpful. I wanted to stall a bit longer before beginning another arduous day, so I heated up more hot water for coffee and sat watching the fog drift across the lake. Everything was peaceful except for a group of Boy Scouts camped on the other end of the lake. Their voices carried clearly across the placid water, and I wanted them to shut the hell up. No chance. Adolescent energy ruled that out. I suppose when I was their age I was probably an irritation to someone at some camping area we shared. Payback is a bitch.

On Day Thirteen, Peter and I broke camp around 9:00 a.m. It was our goal to get through the Goat Rocks Wilderness and over Knife's Edge by the end of the day. But first, we would have to get across more snow in order to reach Cispus Pass. The thought of what lay before me was cause for reasonable anxiety. The trail forward required us to hike across about two hundred yards of a steep snowpack that led to another hundred feet of loose shale and then scramble up the side of the mountain to the pass. This was the second time that a snowpack might create a barrier. About now I was questioning my rationale for failing to include crampons. They weigh less than ten ounces and take minimal space in a pack side pocket. I couldn't come up with any particular reason for their exclusion except I figured a few snowfields wouldn't be a problem to an old, seasoned backpacker like me. Wrong! I made a note in my journal entry at the end of the day to include crampons in any backpack that would take me to an altitude of 4,500 feet or higher. There are some patches of snow that stubbornly remain on the mountains winter after winter. The learning curve in backpacking never ceases.

Within an hour, Peter and I stood at the foot of the narrow trail that led across nearly two hundred feet of snow. I shook my head in disbelief, because it was eight hundred feet down the side of the mountain with nothing to break a quick slide off the slick trail. And, looking up, the way up to the pass was equally steep and forbidding. There was no other option but to take a couple deep breaths, muster a whole lot of courage, and set aside my profound fear of heights. With my pack still on my back, I stood waiting for something to convince me it was time to begin. Peter and his dogs had already started and were about halfway across when I took my first step on the snow. Just then, the group of men we had met the day before came up behind me, so I stepped back off the trail and let them pass. They were a group from Bellevue, Washington. Young, virile, and fearless. I despised them.

Peter couldn't look back to see whether or not I had followed, and I was too far behind for him to help if I got into any trouble. So, taking a few deep breaths and whispering my most earnest prayers, again I stepped out onto the snowy trail. Well, actually, there wasn't a trail as such; there were only boot imprints left by other hikers that led across the side of the mountain. My goal was to step into the imprints, one after the other, but within a short distance I could feel my boots slipping on snow that had turned to ice the previous night and had yet to begin its daily thaw. I stood still for a few seconds, took another deep breath, and gingerly continued. About five steps farther, my feet slipped out from under me. I instinctively twisted my body, falling so that I landed on my butt. Immediately, I began to slide down the side of the mountain. I hastily jammed both feet and trekking poles into the snow to slow my slide. With The Rock strapped securely to my back, I feared I would become an enormous boulder gathering snow and velocity until I flipped over and barreled down the long slope to the rocky bottom. But after about twenty feet, I simply stopped. My stomach, though, accompanied by my pounding heart, continued on down the mountain. I sat where I was, determined not to move an inch, while I tried to collect myself before I went into a panic attack. I heard Peter yell at me to stay put, that he'd make his way down to help me. I yelled back over my shoulder, "What the hell for? I got myself into this mess and it's up to me to figure it out."

After a long minute, I gingerly began to scooch myself upwards towards the spot where I had slipped. I moved gingerly, inch by anxious inch, the entire time saying to myself, "Be calm. You are just fine. This is an adventure." Actually, I was scared shitless, but I dared not acknowledge the fear. In this situation, fear was my enemy. I needed calm and peace. I needed resolve and belief in myself to get out of this mess. So up and up, one inch, two inches, I scooched towards the icy trail of boot prints until I could feel my wet and cold butt on something flat. It was the trail! But the ordeal wasn't over. I sat considering how I was going to hoist myself upward, back on my feet, and get headed the right direction. The Rock was still on my back, so hoisting was not going to be as easy as it seemed. And I had spent so much physical and emotional energy over the last few minutes that I questioned if I had enough reserves to get back on my feet. With a couple deep breaths and a resolve coming from some deep place within, and using my trekking poles as support, I hoisted myself back on my feet. In so doing, I got turned around, headed back from where I had begun! "Oh shit!" I blurted out loud. But, gratefully, I was vertical and not splayed out on some boulder hundreds of feet below.

As it turned out, facing in the "wrong" direction was fortuitous. I needed to return to where I had begun, sit down, and collect myself before attempting the crossing again. By now, Peter had reached the top of the pass and was looking several hundred feet down towards where I was sitting. He yelled to me, "Wait there, I'll come back and get your pack!"

I yelled back, "No way! You stay there and I'll figure this thing out."

I backtracked to the edge of the snowfield, about fifty feet from where I'd slipped, dropped my pack, and collapsed on the soggy ground. After several minutes of rest, I heard footsteps crunching my way. I sat up and looked towards the trail. Someone familiar was crossing the snow towards me. A few yards closer, I realized it was Dan, one of the men I had met the previous day. He had broken away from his group of buddies when he saw what had happened.

"I feel like I'm going to throw up," I said looking up at him.

"That was a rough go back there," he countered in a calm voice. And without another word, he took off his pack and began riffling through it. In a few seconds his hand came out of his pack holding boot crampons. He thrust them towards me. "Here, take these. I don't need them and you sure as hell do."

I put them on and quickly asked, "Where can I meet you on the trail and return them?"

"No need. I own a restaurant in Bellevue, so someday after you've returned, assuming you return," he chuckled, "bring your wife or girlfriend in and return them. I trust you."

I wrote down the name of his restaurant, and with that quick exchange, he turned around and hiked back across the snowfield. The crampons worked, and I was able to get across without further incident and up to Cispus Pass, where I met up with Peter. From his vantage point and to my embarrassment, he had witnessed the entire incident from beginning to end.

"What's this thing with you and snow?" he jabbed at me.

"The snow gods have it out for me. If I die on the PCT, it'll probably be on a damned snowdrift."

Peter and I parted at the top of the Pass. I wanted to take an hour or so to recover from my near-death experience, and he wanted to cover as many miles as he could that day. He still had to get across Goat Rocks Pass and to White Pass to meet his wife, and there was no way I could hike the remaining twenty-two miles by the end of the day. For the third time in as many days, we shook hands, said our farewells, and exchanged addresses. He headed down the side of the pass towards the Goat Rocks Wilderness. I sat under a scrubby pine tree, wrote several pages in my journal, and ate some lunch. It was around noon, and I still had about ten miles of hard hiking to reach Goat Rocks Pass, which was another challenge all its own.

Journal Entry:

Sitting under a scrubby tree that appears to be growing out of solid rock. Made it to the top of Cispus Pass after a harrowing experience that sent me plummeting down the side of the mountain. From where I am sitting I can see where I would have landed...not a pretty sight!

Peter and I said our goodbyes, probably for the last time. He's been a genuine Godsend and I'll miss his company.

I'm still pretty rattled from crossing the snowfield, so will take a few minutes to collect my wits and have an early lunch. It's quiet and all I can hear is a breeze and a distant creek.

I'm feeling a lot of gratitude for all the kindness shown to me over the past couple of days by Peter and others. I did not come to hike the PCT to fail or be harmed.

My frayed faith is restored every day I am on the Trail. Help always seems to show up eventually, and it comes in many forms.

13

SCOUTS ON THE MOUNTAIN

After Peter left, I lay down under a scrubby pine tree, took a full hour to recover, then headed north.

I knew two other men back home who had hiked this part of the PCT, and both were emphatic that I shouldn't attempt to cross Goat Rocks Pass at the end of the day when already fatigued or in the shadows of late afternoon. This particular portion of the PCT raised a lot of concerns, even among the more seasoned hikers. It's a narrow trail, less than two feet wide, that stretches across the tip of Snowy Mountain with steep drops of several hundred feet on either side of the trail. And the trail is less than solid, because about three inches of slippery shale covers its surface. Once on the trail, there is little margin for error. A slip on the shale and a hiker could be sliding a few hundred feet to the bottom. It's a dangerous few miles, requiring caution and full strength.

My main concern was about the encroaching shadows on the trail. I have only one eye, which means that my depth perception often poses a challenge. For the fully sighted hiker, shadows are simply shadows. For a one-eyed hiker, a shadowy trail could mean a two-to-five-inch differential where he places his steps. I didn't need to risk another misstep.

***

In 1994, I experienced a spontaneous retinal detachment. One afternoon while mowing a section of our lawn with my riding mower, I noticed something was amiss about my eyesight. I was seeing about half of what was in front of me. It was if someone had put a piece of duct tape halfway across my right eye. I went up to the house and called my optometrist, told him what I was experiencing, and two hours later was sitting on an operating table at a local hospital while the doctor explained my options for eye surgery.

A year or so after attempting several procedures to save the eye, I had it removed and was fitted with a prosthesis. It was a bitter and difficult choice for me to make: hope and wait for some future medical miracle while continuing with frustration and discomfort, or have the damned thing removed and get on with my life. After weeks of soul-searching and hearing second, third, and fourth opinions, I chose to begin a life with all the challenges that accompany experiencing the world through one eye. Good depth perception requires two good eyes. My kids used to laugh as they watched me attempt to light a candle or pour a glass of milk. It took my brain several years to adjust and not miss everything by several inches. Even today, over twenty years later, depth perception on dark or cloudy days is challenging. So, when I reached Goat Rocks Pass around seven in the evening, when the day-end shadows began to lie across the trail, I felt a marked level of dread. But by the time I had arrived at the pass, there was no turning back. I either camped on a snowfield or committed to hiking the trail across the pass another four to six difficult miles. I chose to trudge on.

***

The hike from Cispus Pass to the beginning of Goat Rocks Pass had been spectacular, though difficult. With stunning views of Mt. Adams, Mt. St. Helens, and Mt. Rainier, I almost forgot how difficult and steep the trail was. In this particular section I met up with about twenty Boy Scouts who were on a fifty-mile hike as part of their requirement towards earning the Eagle Scout Award. They were all in their early- to mid-teens. The oldest, and perhaps the senior scout, looked around seventeen. Our first encounter came when they stopped about two miles from Cispus Pass for a lunch break and were spread out along the trail. As I passed them, it was obvious that most were inexperienced and had come ill-prepared and poorly equipped for such a rigorous hike. A ragtag lot if I ever saw one. As I hiked by, I nodded and said a few "hellos," but didn't feel like stopping. I still had a lot of mileage to cover before the end of the day.

For the next several hours, I passed through fields of bright purple lupine, crossed several gentle creeks being fed by glaciers visible in the distance, and was only a head-turn away from a spectacular view of Mt. Rainier. And as I passed the forty-foot-high Split Rock, I took a few pictures of this rare phenomena to show friends back home. Fortunately, there were ample water sources flowing off the snow packs that also kept the meadows lush with various grasses and wildflowers. The snowfields that stubbornly remained were relatively flat. Nevertheless, I stopped at each to strap on the crampons Dan had lent me. Even on flat snow, having them on the bottoms of my boots gave me greater stability and confidence. Whether on flat terrain or across a steep slope, snow creates another level of physical exertion and difficulty. There is always that split second when a boot can step on an icy patch. Avoiding such a fall takes more energy out of the day's dwindling resources.

By the time I reached a small shelf at the base of Knife's Edge Trail, which leads over Goat Rocks Pass, it was almost 7:00 p.m. About a hundred yards up the trail towards the shelf, I could hear a lot of talking and laughing. The group of Scouts had passed me a few miles back, so I assumed it was them and that they, too, were about to hike across the narrow and sketchy trail. Everything in me screamed this was a very bad idea to begin hiking Knife's Edge this late and weary, but my choices were to either camp in the snow or motor on. I should have camped a mile or so down the trail, but I had come too far to turn back. I figured I could follow them over the pass to whatever camping area became available.

The twenty scouts lying splayed out on the ground with their packs strewn around in no particular order were a sorry sight. Several of the kids had their heads buried in iPhones or whatever item of technology they had brought along to keep connected with the world they had left a few days earlier. A few of the kids were sitting with their backs against rocks, and some were just idly chatting with one another. But there was no quiet or silence among them, and it all thoroughly pissed me off.

I flung The Rock down and stood over the Scouts, watching them involved in everything but what was right in front of them. That giant was looming in the distance so large and majestic it felt as though I could reach out and touch it. I can't remember being so moved by an inanimate object as I was in that moment. So I sat on a rock and just stared at this majestic sight. After about two or three minutes of listening to the Scouts chatter about girls and lack of food and whatever nonsense that came to their minds and watching the several others move their phones around in front of them in hopes of finding enough signal to continue their long-distance conversations, I turned around and blurted out, "What the hell are you guys doing? Do you know you are sitting at the feet of something holy and you're talking about shit?"

A few looked up at me as if to say, "What? What are you talking about?" But I couldn't stop myself. I was still catching my breath from the last few miles of the steep trail that led to where we were gathered. So I was pretty ramped up.

"Hell, it's right in front of you! Mt. Rainier!'

I turned away from them and pointed in the direction of this massive, snow-covered sight. I turned around to face them again.

"Do you know you are probably twenty kids among millions who will ever have the privilege of seeing what you are seeing and you're wasting your time with silliness? Be still and think about this moment that you'll never experience again. Look at that holy mountain and be grateful."

And then I stood up.

Still pretty ramped up, I asked, "Where's your scoutmaster?"

One of the kids answered, "He and his wife are looking for the best route to take over the pass."

"Well, there's the stock route and the hiker's route. It doesn't look as though the stock route is safe enough.

Too steep. Too much snow. You can tell that from where you're sitting."

"Yeah, we told them that, but they wanted to look anyway."

I sat closer to the group. By now I had caught my breath and was feeling a bit calmer. Several of the Scouts were looking at me as I began a conversation with a couple nearest to where I was sitting. I couldn't help but notice their clothing and equipment. I shook my head.

"Did you guys do much planning before you left?"

"Not much. We got a list of stuff we had to bring and we brought as much as we had."

"Yeah, but what about those tennis shoes some of you are wearing? Whoever told you it was okay to hike fifty miles in tennis shoes? Only a couple of you have boots. And who let you on this hike wearing blue jeans? Man, never, never wear cotton in the mountains. It's a surefire pathway to hypothermia."

"I never heard that," another boy responded.

"Anything made of cotton doesn't belong on a hike. Just remember that one thing if nothing else."

I heard a muffled "thanks" coming somewhere from the group.

After those remarks, some of them sort of shuffled around from where they sat. I was chewing on a mouthful of trail mix, and by now most of the kids had put away their phones. In a calmer and more gracious tone, I started up again.

"Listen, you guys, this is a really big deal. I mean, hiking fifty miles as a part of your Eagle Scout Award is really big, but you've got to come better prepared the next time you attempt something like this. Go to REI or go online and do some research about clothing and equipment. You're just damned lucky nothing major has happened so far. And for God's sake, leave your technology behind. When you're backpacking, get unplugged."

Right about then, the two adult leaders appeared and announced to all of us that, because of the snowdrifts, the so-called "stock trail" around the Goat Rocks was too dangerous for foot traffic and we would all have to take the "hiker's trail" on Knife's Edge, the very top of the pass. A few of the kids jumped up and started to gather their gear. I also stood but then asked them to all sit for a minute. The two adults (husband and wife) looked startled by my request, as if I had any authority to speak to the group. And then I said, "Listen, you guys, I didn't mean to sound like a snarly old fart telling you how to do your hike, but it seems to me there's some really basic stuff here you all are missing and that's all I was trying to tell you…aside from all the noise you were making when I reached you."

A few of the kids chuckled. The adults still looked a little surprised, and then I told them what I had said to their troop. "I simply told the kids that right here we were standing on holy ground, and looking out towards Mt. Rainier, we were in the presence of something really special, so messing around with the iPhones and talking smack about one another or girls or whoever's back home is not cool."

I thought for certain the adults would tell me to screw off and mind my own business. Instead the husband said, "Thank you! My wife and I have been trying to tell them those very same things since the day we left. Maybe they'll listen to you."

I felt slightly vindicated.

My unsolicited interchanges with the Scouts brought back memories of my own scouting experiences. But mainly, I thought of Glenn Allen and what he might have said to those boys as they sat around yakking about nothing appropriate for the moment. He would never have allowed them to take anything technological on a backpack. Not even a GPS. "Maps and compasses are all you need," he would assert. "Everything else stays behind." And there would be no negotiation. "We're here to get away from all the trappings of normal life, not bring it with us." I wondered if Glenn was looking down at me smiling and whispering under his heavenly breath, "Halleluiah, he finally got it!"

***

I watched as the kids gathered up stuff they had strewn around their area, strapped on their packs, and headed towards the beginning of Knife's Edge. I decided to stay behind a few minutes and take another long look at the mountain before heading out. I wanted to enjoy it in peace, in a silence I had not been able to enjoy with all the kids present. It was a little after 7:00 p.m., and I knew I had to get going or I could easily be on the pass in the dark. That would be tempting the gods.

The trail along the Goat Rocks Pass is called "Knife's Edge" for good reason. It is a narrow and unstable trail of shale on which a hiker is only one slip from plunging several hundred feet down a steep slope in either direction. I leapfrogged the scout troop. By then I knew a couple of their names, and we had a few friendly exchanges. They were actually a sweet group of kids who were doing their level best to survive a fifty-mile hike. I told several of them that they should take a lot of pride in what they were doing. I think I even told a couple of them I, too, was an Eagle Scout about a hundred years ago. They laughed at my self-deprecation.

***

A new troop was being organized in our neighborhood, and several of my classmates were gung-ho to join. So, not to be left out of all the excitement of new beginnings, cool uniforms, the opportunity to advance in status, and earn merit badges to be worn boldly for all to see and praise, I joined. This had all the makings of my kind of club. At first I relished it. But more and more it felt too restrictive, like an extension of home and school where there were expectations to perform and achieve. And there was always someone in uniform yelling at me to do something different or better than I had already done. At some point, the scouting experience ceased being fun. But I persevered and continued on a fast track to become an Eagle Scout. At the time, I didn't have any concept about its importance. I think I continued primarily because it pleased my otherwise silent and distant stepfather, and because he, too, had been a Boy Scout. I don't remember him telling me much about his own experiences, but I do remember he was quite enthusiastic about mine. So I stuck with it and quickly made my way up the ranks while collecting copious merit badges that, upon earning, my mother immediately sewed on my sash.

Then, one spring just two weeks before the ceremony to award me and two others our Eagle Scout Award, and three months before our troop was headed for Valley Forge, Pennsylvania to attend the National Boy Scout Jamboree, our scoutmaster absconded with all the funds our troop had worked to earn towards that trip. So, with no leadership, no funds, utterly dismayed at the unfairness of it all, with broken faith and a broken heart, I left the Boy Scouts and never looked back—and never received the Eagle Scout Award I thought I really deserved.

Later that summer, at the invitation of a school chum, I joined the local YMCA on a backpack into the High Sierras. My loyalties immediately shifted and I came home from those eight days in the mountains, gathered up all my Scout paraphernalia—the uniforms, the merit badges, the medals, and certificates—put them into a box, and placed it with that week's trash collection. Until just recently, I had never regretted that decision. But it was a significant achievement in the early years of my life, and now I would have liked some record to show for all that effort.

And from time to time, I do wonder whatever became of that son of a bitch who stole our troop's money.

***

As I had feared, the sun was fading into dusk and I would soon to be hiking in the dark, and at 6,500 feet, the temperature had dropped significantly enough that many of us had stopped to put on warmer clothes. All of us, including the young, virile Scouts, were bushed. We had all hiked across Cispus Pass that morning and had survived the risks involved. Even they had difficulty with the snow and steepness of the trail. But the Goat Rocks Wilderness was a different challenge, and crossing Old Snowy on the narrow path of Razor's Edge was not for the faint-hearted. Hiking on shale is a little like walking on a path of broken dishes. And it was getting darker by the minute. I remained at the back of the group, where a couple of the kids lingered a little behind to make certain I was keeping up. It was nothing spoken, but I understood their kind intentions. I didn't tell anyone the reason for my poor night vision, nor did I mention my COPD.

It was about 8:30 p.m. and getting darker by the minute when we finally got across the pass and came to a place flat enough for camping. The area was also littered with shale, but at least it was flat and there were a few spots where the dirt showed through the shale and tent spikes could be pounded into the ground.

By the time I found a spot to pitch my tent, about as far as I could get from the Scouts, it was around 9:30 p.m. and completely dark, save the sight of a few flashlights the Scouts were waving around in their own campsites about a hundred feet away from mine. I was drenched in perspiration, becoming more chilled by the minute, and a bit shaky from hunger. As I set about getting all my equipment out of my pack and looking for a spot to pitch the tent, I saw a woman come towards me from about twenty feet away. She held a flashlight to light up the ground and as she came closer called out, "Hey, we just saw you guys come off the pass. Man, what a bitch."

"No kidding," I responded without looking up.

She stood silently while holding her flashlight on my area so I could get the tent pitched and find all the things I needed to get my stove lit and some water boiled for dinner. She continued to stand nearby with the flashlight on me as I kept readying things for dinner, getting my sleeping bag tucked into the tent, and removing my sweaty shirt to put on some thermo clothes. When she seemed content that I was settled in, she excused herself and walked away towards her own tent. By then I had my headlamp turned on to light my area. In my haste to get things accomplished, I hadn't even asked her name or anything about her. She just appeared, welcomed me, and offered some assistance.

I ate a quick dinner and got into bed as soon as things were put away. That night, after the most challenging and frightening day on the PCT, I said prayers of gratitude for safety and for all the people who were my Angels. But a few more days like Cispus Pass and Goat Rocks Wilderness and I'd be ready to beat a quick retreat towards home. Frederick Nietzsche claimed that what didn't kill us would make us stronger. I don't think Fred ever hiked along Knife's Edge or climbed across the snow bank up to Cispus Pass.

14

THE KRACKER BARREL

I have spent most of my life setting goals, realizing a few, missing the mark on most, making excuses for some, and girding my loins to complete the rest. Even in play, I am an adamant goal-setter. I suppose that is why I was attracted to running marathons and other shorter distances. A certain distance to run in a certain timeframe is the perfect sport for someone like me because there is no bullshitting the clock. I was only as good as the clock told me. The clock kept me honest. But on the PCT, there are no clocks and no particular markers between one day to the next, and no one was on the sidelines or at the finish mark tracking my success or failure.

Journal Entry:
I have made a conscious decision to set aside any written-in-stone goals. I have removed my watch and stuck it in a side pocket of my backpack and will rarely pay attention to the time of day.

Almost every day I have met hikers who are hell-bent to complete a twenty-five-to-forty-mile day. I even met someone who was attempting to set a new PCT speed record. I could barely get my head around such a goal. Setting a speed record on a trail this abundant with beauty and lushness, replete with streams and meadows and rock formations, seems almost sacrilegious.

Every day is a fresh opportunity to experience nature's treasures. Why would anyone want to rush through all of this? And yet, some do. I am not going to be among them. It is a sobering thing to understand that I will never pass this way again. So I will take each day as it comes. I will stop when it pleases me to sit beside a clear, bubbling creek with water so cold it will hurt my teeth. I will sit and chew on some particle of food while I take in a glorious view of majestic mountains. I will doff my clothes and plunge into an inviting mountain lake so cold it might yank the breath right out of my throat. I will take the time to visit with anyone I meet along the trail who wants to sit awhile and swap stories. And I will end the day when it feels just right to do so, no matter how far I have come that day. I will stop in time to gather wood for the evening's campfire, and I will take off my boots, boil water for a cup of tea, and light a cigar if there is one to smoke. I will sit and look out at the beauty right in front of me, write in my journal, perhaps watch the sunset, and be grateful for the peace and quiet of the wilderness that surrounds me. What has been chasing me for a lifetime or whatever it was I have been chasing, I will not bring here. And so if someone boasts of his or her thirty-mile day of hiking, I will be at peace with the far lesser miles I hiked that day. I've spent most my life in a rush, trying to prove to someone or myself that I was worthy. I will spend this extraordinary time on the PCT at my own pace. And I will arrive every day at exactly the place I need to be. And each day I will say a prayer of gratitude.

***

On Day Thirteen, I lay snug in my bag, in no hurry to climb out of my tent into a cold, foggy morning. Some of the PCT hikers would be on the trail by five in the morning, still dark, hiking with headlamps lighting up the early-morning trail. My tent entrance was still zipped closed, so I couldn't see whether or not the Scouts had left. I figured they hadn't since I'd heard no noises coming from where they were camped. They were a very noisy bunch, so I knew they were still in the sack and would get a later start. I didn't want to be leapfrogging them all day, so I decided to get up and get on the trail.

I was sitting crouched by my stove, waiting for the water to boil, when I saw the woman from last night make her way towards me. I stood and greeted her with an apology that I hadn't even asked her name or inquired anything about her the previous night. What I said didn't seem particularly funny, but even so she let out a very loud laugh.

"Honey, you looked so beat I thought I'd have to cook your dinner and feed you myself!" We both laughed.

My water was boiling and we squatted down next to my stove as I began to spoon out some coffee crystals from a plastic bag. Quickly, she told me to stop, reached into her jacket pocket, pulled out a handful of Starbucks coffee packages, and handed them to me. Wow!

"My friend and I are getting off the trail a few miles north of here and heading home. We won't be needing these. They'll taste better than that crap you brought along." This time my expressions of gratitude were profuse. We sat together as I sipped that lovely cup of Starbucks coffee.

Betty and her lifelong friend lived on the East Coast and had talked about hiking in the Washington Cascades since they were children. She told me neither of their husbands had wanted to make the trip, so they'd made this their own adventure. They had hiked about fifty miles, with about five miles to go to the spur trail leading back to their car. It had been everything they had hoped it would be. I suppose I could have foregone that second cup of coffee, packed up, and gotten a head start on another day of difficult hiking. But then I would have missed hearing this wonderful story of the two women whose friendship began as little girls, meeting in a Baptist Sunday school room, and spanned over fifty years, now older women realizing their childhood dream of a long hike in the Cascades. As I finished my coffee, Betty walked back to her camp area to begin preparations to get back on the trail. She, too, expressed a desire to get ahead of the Scouts.

I could see from where I was sitting that the Scouts were beginning to rise and come to life. I wanted to get as far ahead of them as I could for a few hours of peace and quiet before they inevitably caught up with me by midmorning. It appeared that Betty and her friend were thinking the same thing. They both hurriedly stuffed their backpacks in preparation for a quick retreat. I was ready before them, and, as I passed them, expressed more thanks for the coffee, adding, "I think you gals are amazing, and you probably had a better time without your husbands!"

"Damned straight we did!" Betty quickly shot back at me with a loud chuckle.

***

The next day, Day Fourteen, I was sitting about ten feet from the shore of Gillette Lake drinking a cup of Starbucks coffee made from one of Betty's packages. The previous day had been among the most difficult, with too many switchbacks, more snowfields, and swampy meadows that were breeding grounds for pesky insects. I had wanted to complete the fifteen miles to White Pass but simply ran out of steam. After about thirteen miles, I found a perfect campsite a few feet from Gillette Lake. I was the only person on the lake, so with just me and the sound of frogs and gentle breezes coming off the water, Gillette Lake was all mine.

I had hiked about 160 miles in two weeks, with one zero day in Trout Lake. It was about 8:00 a.m. I had finished breakfast, packed up most of my equipment, and was sitting watching a few ripples on the placid lake that a trout had created in its quest for a morning bug. I was in no hurry to put The Rock on my back, but I was excited to collect my next reload box from home. Excitement ruled. I gulped down my last swallow of coffee, stuffed the cup in a side pocket of my pack, and headed on the trail towards White Pass.

***

The Kracker Barrel was another designated place where PCT hikers could receive reload packages. It is a gas station and general store with a few tables inside to sit at and munch on whatever junk food is available. I chose some nameless bakery item with enough chemicals to guarantee a fifty-year shelf life and two small cartons of chocolate milk. Several other PCT hikers were seated in the area, all eating items we would not be caught dead eating back home. A few of the hikers had done all 160 miles from the Columbia Gorge to White Pass without a resupply break at Trout Lake. As it turned out, a couple of the hikers weren't even aware that there was such a place as Trout Lake and were totally stunned that they had hiked so many miles when they could have split up their mileage on this section. Whatever their reasons for missing out on Trout Lake, I was smugly delighted I had made that choice. I could never have carried enough food for a two-week hike, and a ten-to-fourteen-day stretch may have proved more than I could have endured.

The woman behind the counter asked if anyone wanted to use the washer and dryer while we were just sitting around. I had forgotten that White Pass was among the few places where a hiker could do laundry. I waited the appropriate few seconds before raising my hand with a shout of, "I do!"

I unloaded all of my clothes from my pack, took off my shirt and socks, and headed back to use the machines. For five bucks, with soap provided, I washed and dried all my clothes. There are few things sweeter in a long-distance hike than clean clothes, even though some of my clothes would never be really "clean" again. But this would do. And besides, "clean" is relative. "Good enough" is a theme that would have brought exceedingly more peace to my life had I embraced it as a young man. And now, if I could only remember that, I'd live a happier life.

I spent the rest of the morning in simple pleasures: chatting with various other PCT hikers, eating inordinate amounts of junk food, and staying off my feet as much as possible to give my aching, blistered feet a needed rest.

It was midday and I was sitting at one of the picnic tables at the back of the store with about five other hikers when I heard familiar noises. I slipped on my sandals and headed around the corner to the front of the building. There they were—my Scout buddies. All twenty of them and all looking about as ragged and weary and beat-up as any group of hikers I had ever witnessed. They immediately noticed me and a couple came up to me with big bear hugs. They smelled like pig shit!

"Where the hell you guys been? I thought you'd be hours in front of me."

"We misread the map and took a spur trail that led to nowhere. Cost us about five hours of hiking, so we made camp about eight miles from here."

"What? No map readers among you?" I chided them. "Well, I'm glad you're safe, and what the hell, you finished your fifty miles. Wrong spur or not, you did it."

"No more long hikes for this Scout," one of the kids murmured.

One of the older Scouts with whom I had had several short conversations over the past couple days left the group to go into the store. I followed him. He and another of the older kids were standing by the door waiting to use the bathroom at the back of the store. I told them I was really proud of their achievement.

"I will promise you something that I want you to remember. And when it happens, I will be long in the grave. But I want you to think about this: You will be at your high school twentieth reunion and you will not speak about who won what football game or who got to go to the prom with Becky What's-Her-Name or who lost their virginity at the all-night party. You will seek one another out and you will share stories about this amazing fifty-mile experience. And you might remember the old fart who jumped up your ass about not taking the moment more seriously, the old man who said something about being on holy ground and wearing all the wrong stuff and not wearing cotton on a backpack."

Right then, one of the boys looked up and saw the bathroom was available. But I plowed on, and he stayed.

"Listen, this might be the most important thing you will ever do in your youth. So just give yourselves a great big pat on your backs and celebrate this moment."

Either out of fatigue or a genuine sense of the importance of that moment, we three stood looking at one another with teary eyes, and I ended my speech with a hug for them both.

Then the taller and older of the two said, "A bunch of us talked about you after we separated. We didn't know if we'd ever see you again. Some of the guys were kidding that you were some kind of mystic who just appears here and there around the mountain. But I figured I'd see you again." The words barely out of his mouth, and we were laughing. It was a good moment between us.

I could hear the creaking of the bathroom door as it opened. A Scout walked out and barked, "Next!" And one of the boys standing with me turned around to take his turn. I walked out of the store towards my pack at the side of the building. I had just poured a cup of the freshly brewed coffee into my favorite cup, so I sat on the table and watched a couple other hikers repack their packs now that they had also collected their reload boxes. I was in no hurry to do much of anything, so sitting and watching was just fine with me. The longer I stayed on the trail, the easier just doing nothing became.

I didn't see the Scouts leave but suspected that at least one of them had called home up the trail from Highway 12. Their rides had arrived to take them home. I was a little sad to see the Scouts leave. Even with all their goofiness and my intrusive lectures, their presence on the trail added several quirky moments and conversations that often brought smiles to our faces and some laughter. In those three days of intermittent connections, quite surprisingly, I think we grew on each other.

I finished my coffee and went looking for the public phone. Back home I had decided that carrying a cell phone on the trail was just a nuisance with extra weight. In fact, it's a nuisance at any time, and besides, on the trail it was a rarity to get any reception. I didn't locate the public phone, so asked the clerk in the store. "Oh, we had that taken out several years ago. Vandals would just break into it and try to take the coins. Sorry."

Sorry, my ass, I needed to call my wife and tell her I'd just finished my first 160 miles. I wanted to share my wonderful success and receive a few kudos. I wanted some praise and verbal backslapping. What the hell! No one around me was using a cell phone, so it wasn't as though I could ask to borrow a phone. There were no phones. After a few minutes of frustration and getting more comfortable with the fact that I was truly out of communication with my family, I settled into a calmer sense that Carla would know I was okay and that if anything adverse happened to me, someone would contact her. I carried ample identification and, besides, I wore a green, rubber identification bracelet on my left wrist with my name and Carla's phone number stamped on it. It was a gift from my daughter and her caring contribution to my wilderness experience.

15

FOOTSORE

In the jargon of the PCT hiker, a "rest day" is referred to as a "zero day." Typically they are taken at the place where reload boxes are collected, laundry is done, and coin-operated showers are taken. I took one zero day in Trout Lake and one at White Pass. I could easily have taken more and benefited. By now, blisters were copious and my right foot ached beyond the help of ibuprofen. In the world of "pain scaling," my feet were a solid seven or eight out of ten, with no relief on the horizon. This was my first inkling that I may have selected and been sold the wrong boot for this particular hike. Usually I accept the advice of folks who work at REI, but in the matter of my boots, I think I should have sought further counsel. While one boot may be appropriate for a particular kind of hiking, another may not. Most of my backpacks had been five to ten days or day hikes in the eight-to-twelve-mile range. The PCT was a totally different matter. Day after day of fifteen to twenty miles carrying a forty-pound pack required a boot that I was not wearing. Too late. I would simply have to make do. But I planned to have a serious conversation with the management at the REI store where I'd purchased my boots the past spring.

When the salesperson heard me tell of my plans to hike the PCT, I wish a light had gone on in his head that told him the boot I was considering was not the best boot for my purposes. I needed a less flexible and a sturdier boot given the mileage and the weight of my pack. I wondered if that was simply another form of being "invisible." I had an unsettling thought: Did my age cause him to doubt my serious intent to hike several hundred miles a few months later? I hoped not, but sensed otherwise.

***

As a section hiker, covering vast distances each day to reach a particular goal was not as essential to me as it might be for the thru hiker whose ultimate goal was to get ahead of any bad weather on their way to Canada. Those thru hikers traveling from Canada to Mexico had to pass through the High Sierras before the fall snows commenced. I could afford a zero day or two to nap, read, devour extra calories, write in my journal, sit by a campfire and chat it up with others, take a quick swim in a nearby lake, and pamper my blistery and aching feet. I was determined not to let myself get twisted up about time. My hike and my journey wasn't just about walking a certain number of miles, it was also about staying in place, enjoying the solitude. And that is what I did at White Pass. I found a perfect campsite next to Leach Lake about four hundred yards north of where I had stopped for my reload package. It was within a short walking distance of the Kracker Barrel, where I could get a decent cup of coffee or a tolerable slice of pizza fresh out of the oven. I could also sit at one of the small tables, write in my journal, and share trail stories with other PCT hikers who had arrived for their boxes and were also taking a zero day.

By this point, the majority of those I met were from the East Coast who had hiked the Appalachian Trail or the Continental Divide in past years. They would often make comparisons between their experiences on those trails, and the PCT usually won out when it came to splendid views, grandeur, and levels of difficulty. Most of the hikers I met were students with freshly minted degrees and no sense of what their next plunge into a vast sea of possibilities would entail. Some were experiencing levels of career uncertainty and taking time away from the daily grind to ponder a different future. Mostly, though, the PCT hikers I met were simply fulfilling some lifelong dream and the challenge of hiking the 2,700 miles from Mexico to Canada. Life, as they had known it, could be shelved for a few months. Invariably I would suggest, "Life will be waiting for you when you return and then you get to work for the next forty years."

Groans usually followed those remarks.

"Take this time while you can."

Someone responded, "I wish my dad had that thought!"

I could usually get a pass on what advice or responses I gave because I was always the oldest and often the one with the most backpacking experience. This was nothing to brag about, but it did give me a perspective that younger or less-experienced hikers lacked.

What I had observed over the past couple of weeks was the disparity of age groups. Here's the breakdown I noted: The majority of the hikers were between twenty and twenty-five, with a smattering of those in their early thirties, then the age group seemed to leap into folks in their early to mid-fifties. Thus far I had not met anyone in their sixties, and I was the only hiker in the seventies range. My age and the fact that I planned to hike through the Washington section—the most difficult—seemed to astonish most people I met.

I also noticed the number of women hiking alone. More were hiking solo than with friends or partners. But most of the men I met were with girlfriends or wives or with a group of other men. I met more solo women hikers than solo men. I don't have any theory about why this was, but it made me think of the concern of folks back home who expressed fears that hiking alone might not be safe. None of the women I met expressed any fears or concerns for their safety. At least not to me. They all seemed pretty self-confident and bold.

16

NORTH TO WILLIAM O. DOUGLAS WILDERNESS

<u>Journal Entry:</u>
Early morning on Day Sixteen and time to head north, leave Leach Lake and the good folks at the Kracker Barrel behind. I could easily spend another day hanging around this place, but when I take extra days to rest, I want it be somewhere a little more remarkable.

The lake is exceedingly buggy, not too inviting for swimming, and there are a couple groups of PCT hikers who plan to stay another day and they are driving me a bit nuts with their noise. Although they are camped several yards away in another area, their voices carry across the quiet forest and placid lake. Time to head out. I am packed and ready to leave but think I'll walk back the few hundred yards to the Kracker Barrel for one last cup of freshly brewed coffee and a couple poppy-seed muffins. And I want to say goodbye to the two women who are running the place and have been so hospitable.

I paid for my coffee and muffins and said my farewells, then sat at one of the empty tables. I was looking over what I had written earlier in my journal when in came a man looking to be in his mid-to-late fifties. I remembered seeing him in Trout Lake but had not met him. He poured a cup of coffee, grabbed something from the bakery shelf, and sat down at the table nearest me. We started up a conversation.

"I'm 'Picks Up Stones," he offered without hesitation. "What's your trail name?"

"Don't have one, yet," I told him, "but I'll have to think of one since everyone I meet asks me."

Then he explained that a PCTer doesn't name himself. A person's trail name is typically chosen by someone else, someone they have met or are hiking with. It is like an anointment that speaks to whom that person is at that moment in time, unlike a birth name that rarely says what is to come. Picks Up Stones had been so named because he'd spent his professional life teaching high school geology.

After several minutes of small talk, I managed to think of at least one question relevant to his expertise: "So, tell me, what's with all that ash I've been stepping in since the Columbia Gorge? I haven't noticed any burn areas, but was there some big fire over the past few years?"

"Nope, but that's what most people think. Actually, it's remnants of the Mt. St. Helen's blast back in the early 80s."

And then I remembered about the only time I knew of Carla ever backpacking.

"My wife was backpacking with some friends on Mt. Hood when she witnessed Mt. St. Helen's blowing."

"And she lived to tell about it?" responding with a surprised look.

"I think I remember her telling me her friends were still in their tents asleep, but she was already up drinking coffee and looking out towards the northwest. She shouted at the others to get up and see what was happening. I think they made a fast retreat back down the mountain."

"Well, a lot of folks weren't so lucky. Actually, had the wind been blowing in her direction, she probably wouldn't have gotten off Mt. Hood."

I made a mental note to myself to share this conversation with Carla when I returned home.

Picks Up Stones was a thru hiker but, due to some family crisis, had to leave the trail and head back home with the hope he could continue his hike when things got settled. He wasn't the first or the last thru hiker I met who left the trail for one reason or another only to return days or weeks later to resume their trek. Only one time did I meet someone who got off the trail with no plans to return. They had simply "had enough of it."

Picks Up Stones finished his coffee and headed towards the parking lot. I could see from where I was sitting his ride had arrived to take him where he needed to go. So I went back to reviewing my journal and making further entries before I, too, headed back to the trail.

***

It wasn't until the next year, while hiking the Oregon portion of the PCT, that I was finally given my trail name. After less than a week of hiking in northern California and several days south of the Oregon border, someone asked me my trail name while standing with a group of other PCTers outside the Hikers Hut in Etna, California.

"Oh, just call me Glenn," was my normal response.

Someone standing next to me blurted out, "Okay, that's your trail name, 'Just Glenn.' We'll call you Just Glenn." Just like that, I had a trail name! And that was good enough for me. At least he didn't name me Methuselah. And the meaning of my trail name is up for grabs. Does it mean, "Just call me Glenn?" or "It's just Glenn hiking alone?" Maybe both. Either way, I had a trail name for the remainder of the Oregon section. I had been baptized into the fellowship of legitimate PCTers!

***

<u>Journal Entry:</u>
Ask Carla about her experience on Mt. Hood.

Ah, the journal. I resisted the idea of keeping one. It seemed like it would be just another hassle and even a bit self-absorbing. There have been times I nearly ditched it for the sake of simplicity because it sometimes seems to be one more thing I need to keep track of and another few ounces that I really don't want to carry. But right now I'm glad I've kept it because every day has not been the same as the last, and at some point in the future, that's something I want to remember.

I don't want to forget that each day is separate, with its meanings and challenges, and its delights and lessons. Yes, there are dozens of lakes and valleys and streams and mountain peaks and flower-covered slopes, but each has its own uniqueness, and though it would take a certified, world-class poet to describe what I witness, I am satisfied with my own limited vocabulary and descriptions. Thus, I keep this journal so that I will remember each day. Still, though, there are times when it is a chore. And during the course of a day, when I do remember to write something, I try not to take a shortcut.

***

I said my goodbyes and headed back to the campsite at Leach Lake where I had left my pack. My next reload box was a hundred miles north at Snoqualmie Pass along Highway 90. Again, because I had loaded all my new provisions for the next leg of the hike, The Rock had returned to its oppressive, excessive weight. I calculated it was somewhere around forty-five pounds.

On the map, the trailhead looked to be within a few yards of where I had camped, but after about fifteen minutes, I still couldn't locate it. I took off my pack and began a more thorough search of the various spots the trail should begin. No luck. I finally did locate a trail and, leaving my pack behind, headed in its direction for a few hundred yards to be certain I had chosen correctly. I walked about a half a mile without seeing any signage on any trees or spur trails. It looked to be headed in the right direction, but something in my gut told me I was on the wrong trail headed the wrong way. So I returned to where I had left The Rock and, with a loud grunt, hoisted it onto my back, fastened and pulled all the appropriate straps, and headed in a direction that looked more promising.

Within a few steps, I sighted a broken piece of signage on a tree barely visible from where I had just been. But there it was. I had lost about two hours searching for the goddamned trailhead! I had actually taken a horse trail that ran somewhat parallel to the PCT but would have eventually taken me eastward rather the northward. I suppose, had I been carrying a GPS, I could have found the trail sooner, but then again, "finding" the trail seemed far more adventurous and daring then just looking at a screen that told me where to go. The "old-fashioned way" of hiking might take longer and create greater margins for error, but it also allowed some level of celebration for discovery. I wasn't sure what or who to be pissed at, the PCT Association for not being more diligent in providing better signage or me for not carrying along more accurate maps or guides. Neither really mattered because I still had a hell of a long and difficult day ahead of me, and there was nothing to be gained by walking the rest of the day in a state of annoyance. I needed all that energy to meet the challenges the day would bring.

Nevertheless, the trail immediately headed up and up and up. After about two miles of a trail that was congested with roots and rocks, a windy and muddy stretch began. At one point I looked down to make certain I wasn't about to trip over a rock imbedded in the path and saw a bright yellow M&M. At first, I thought someone had simply dropped it from their hand as they walked. But then, I saw another, this time bright green, and then another, bright blue. For the next several miles, I realized that someone, for reasons that escape me to this day, had carefully and intentionally dropped M&Ms along the trail. It wasn't as if it was a difficult path to follow. I giggled to myself at the probability of running into Hansel and Gretel making their way back home out of the forest. It was a strange and whimsical thing to do, and I suspected that the person dropping the small pieces of candy had a quirky sense of humor. I hoped it made his/her day a little lighter and more gleeful. It certainly did mine. Even so, given the extra time sipping coffee at the Kracker Barrel and looking for the trail, I figured I had lost about three hours of hiking time. And given the severity of the elevation climb for the day, there was no way I could make up that time. The weight of my pack, my blistered feet, and my own level of strength and hiking stride even on my best days were not going to allow for making up three hours.

The map showed there were a few lakes twelve miles up the trail. It was about 11:00 a.m., and I figured if I kept a fairly steady pace I could make that distance by around 7:00 p.m. That would still give me two hours of daylight, time to gather some wood, make camp, and fix dinner. I felt a sense of giddiness at my renewed goals for the day. And I was pleased I had found the trail. All was not lost and my annoyance of a few hours of lost time soon vanished. That day, like most days on the trail, was an exercise in recalibration and humility. Holding on to any pissiness had no value. Literally and otherwise, each and every day I simply needed to move on. And it was another milestone in my trail reflections to realize I needed to abandon any quest for perfection or, for God's sake, greatness. I needed to get comfortable with simply being normal, and on the PCT, from time to time, it was normal to screw up.

Around noon the trail passed about fifty yards from Deer Lake. I had already passed Sand Lake and Beach Lake and a couple smaller, unnamed lakes. Deer Lake was a fairly large, dark blue, beautiful body of water. I figured this would be a good place to stop for lunch, even though I had only been hiking a little over an hour. My stomach didn't give a hoot how far I had hiked. It told me to stop and fill it. And so I did. I was the only person at the lake, so had another peaceful meal except for all the squirrels and birds doing what they do naturally. I was surprised there weren't any other people enjoying this perfect camping spot on such a hot day. Then it came to me: It was Monday, and most folks were starting a new week of work, including Carla, who I wished could be by my side. Were she here, one of us would dare the other to jump into the lake and test the water. I took a mental note that this was one of the places we should choose as a day hike sometime in the near future.

Around 6:00 p.m. I started looking for Snow Lake. According to my map, I should already have come upon it. It was several yards off the trail, but for a lake that large, it would be hard to miss. Again, my calculations were not in accord with my map. Or, just as probable, my expectation to hike faster and farther than I had had not been realized. According to my body and my aching feet, I should have been at Snow Lake about an hour earlier. According to reality, I would get to Snow Lake when I had covered the required mileage.

No cheating here just because I wanted the lake to make its appearance. Less than a half an hour after accepting my miscalculations, I saw Snow Lake about a hundred yards off to my right. I'd found an absolutely beautiful place and, again, I was the only person within sight. I pitched my tent on a perfectly flat and open camping area about ten feet from the water, and I followed my usual day-end routine. I had found a certain comfort in keeping to a routine. I enjoyed the surprises that each day brought. But at the end of the day, I wanted simplicity.

I sat on the pine-needle-layered ground with my back up against a tree and thought about the morning and how pissed I had been about taking that horse trail a mile out of my way before finding the PCT trailhead. But then I realized, had I actually had those extra hours to hike, I would not have stopped at this place and I wouldn't be sitting here with my cup of tea, looking across this beautiful, calm lake, enjoying the quiet and the solitude. Things do have a way of working out. This was just another lesson for me: to take what comes and enjoy the moment. I think I've been hearing about that sort of life philosophy for the past five decades. Being on the trail, this lesson had begun to make some sense in a practical way.

After dinner I smoked one of the crappy cigars I had purchased at the Kracker Barrel, sat by the small campfire, and began writing.

Journal Entry:
Met several thru hikers today. Tried to be cordial but they were in such a hurry they just blasted by me on their way to complete thirty miles.

My pack strap isn't functioning properly, so my pack isn't snug in the right places. Dragging on my lower back. A new place on my body that aches! Shit!

I'm actually grateful and pleased I got a late start or I would never have had this time right here at this amazing place.

Met a mother and daughter today about six miles north of White Pass on a fifteen-mile day hike. The daughter had thru hiked last year and wanted to show her mother some of what she had experienced. She will be a freshman at Whitman College this fall. I told her about Noah.

Very, very buggy here, but my cigar smoke keeps most the bugs at bay. It works better than oily repellent.

My plan is to hike fifteen miles tomorrow if all goes well and I can keep on the trail and not get sidetracked.

After I finished making several other entries into my journal, I headed for bed. It had been a long day of early frustration and difficult hiking. I didn't make the miles I had planned, but I had hiked what was needed.

***

My daily goal was to be on the trail by 7:00 a.m., but no matter how fast I fixed breakfast or how efficiently I packed up my tent and sleeping bag and the rest of my gear, I rarely got on the trail before 7:30 a.m. Typically around 8:00 a.m. Unless I started the day earlier, I wasn't going to get on the trail much earlier, and I wasn't willing to get out of a warm sleeping bag to gain an hour of hiking. Besides, an extra half hour wasn't going to matter that much in a day of hiking. If I felt so compelled, I could make up the time by taking fewer breaks and a shorter lunch on any given day. That rarely happened.

It was Day Seventeen, and with a hot cup of coffee in hand, I sat on a nearby log and simply watched the stillness of the lake. The bugs had yet to discover my presence, or perhaps they, too, found no sense in rising too early. Nevertheless, I enjoyed the crisp, peaceful morning with the early sky so blue it looked like a movie backdrop. Thus far, I had been blessed with perfect weather. Since the day I started, there hadn't been a single cloud in the sky. Sitting on the log, I announced, out loud, that this day would be a perfect day for a hike, and I would make the fifteen miles I planned. I wanted to camp at Anderson Lake about five miles south of Chinook Pass.

I arrived at Bumping Creek and Packer's Camp around 10:00 a.m. I had hiked the six miles in about two and a half hours, better time than expected. The raging creek had a funky log for a bridge. It was wet and slippery, and no way would I be able to walk across it without falling into the creek, which was waist-deep and fairly swift. After standing on the water's edge for several minutes and weighing my options—fall in and get everything wet or wade across the creek and get just my pants, socks, and boots wet—I decided to skip the crude bridge and pick my way across the stream. I managed to get across without incident. Once on the other side, I removed my boots and socks and set them in a sunny spot to dry. My pants could dry on their own with me in them.

Packer's Camp is a large area where hunters could camp during deer season and where they could tie up their horses and mules before heading into the mountains for the day's hunt. Of course, at this time of year, it was totally empty of any stock or hunters. While my boots and socks were drying, I took the opportunity to fill my water bottles and enjoy a snack. Snacks consisted of trail mix, beef jerky, a candy bar, or one of the several sorts of breakfast or protein bars I had packed. Usually it was whatever I grabbed first out of the food bags in my pack. Typically, I wasn't that particular.

After nearly an hour of waiting, my socks were still too wet to put back on, and wearing wet socks was a surefire guarantee for more blisters. So I pulled out my only other pair of socks and fastened the wet pair to the back of my pack so they could dry over the course of the day. The boots were still fairly wet, but there was nothing I could do about that. At least my socks were dry, and besides, I had already spent an hour at Packer's Camp and it was time to get back on the trail.

It was close to noon and I had not seen any other hikers thus far. I liked the idea that I had the entire forest all to myself. There were those days I just didn't want to meet anyone or tell my story or explain why I didn't have a trail name or hear him exclaim how amazing it was to hike the PCT at my age. For the present, the wilderness was all mine!

For the remainder of the day, the trail was up and down, but mostly up, mostly switchbacks, and mostly hot. But it was also a day of walking through fields of asters, corn lilies, and deep-purple lupines. And a view of Mt. Rainer seldom left my sight. I must have stopped over twenty times to take pictures that I knew I would probably never save. Still, I wanted something to remind me that I had truly been to these places and witnessed such astonishing beauty. It was a day of long mileage, but I was determined to make camp at Anderson Lake.

Anderson Lake was small, calm, and serene. The shore was sandy and, had it been earlier in the day and had I the energy, I would have dived in for a quick swim. But it was 7:00 p.m., the sun was dipping over the mountains, and the air was getting cooler by the minute. So I set up camp, gathered some wood, and fixed my dehydrated Mountain House dinner of beef stroganoff. It had been a long day of hiking and I had kept a pretty decent pace, so I was weak from hunger.

The Mountain House dehydrated packets are among the best things that have come into the backpacker's life: boil two cups of water, pour it into the packet, and wait for about ten minutes. Viola! Dinner is ready. The only downside is that they're only about 500 calories, and after a long day of hiking, that's not sufficient. So I would supplement with more trail mix or protein bars. Before these nifty packages arrived on the scene, a hiker would have to create his own fare, and many still do.

In past years I would pack various rice and soup mixtures. But they couldn't take more than about five minutes to prepare because I wouldn't want to use too much fuel. But the Mountain House meals were so quick and easy. And, yes, after several weeks of the same selections—beef stew, beef stroganoff, Asian chicken and rice, or lasagna—dinner became pretty monotonous. But, then again, after twelve hours of hiking, I had no energy or desire to get fancy about dinner.

After dinner I broke out a couple candy bars and, with a cup of tea, sat back against a large boulder, fed a few sticks to my small campfire, and giggled at how pleased I was for such a good day of hiking. For the entire day, I met only two hikers. They were brothers that had started three months earlier in Compo, California, the south-to-north starting point on the PCT. Alvin and Charles were in their mid-twenties, Charles being the elder by three years. They were from Georgia and, until hiking the PCT, had never been west of St. Louis. They had managed to hike all that distance and were still speaking!

Either one could be a stand-up comedian. They engaged in lots of verbal sparring and were interested that I hiked alone. We sat for an hour and ate a simple lunch together before they headed on their way. The rest of the day was quiet and contemplative, allowing hours of reflection and recollection of memories. I rarely think about my brother, but that day I did. I wondered what it would have been like had he lived and had we shared this experience together.

***

Gaylord was two years my senior. I hold vague and scattered memories of our young lives together. What memories I do recall of our adolescence and young adulthood are not pleasant, and I am hard-pressed to think of a time when we were buddies. Unlike the two brothers from Georgia, we certainly never shared a hike together.

He and I couldn't have been more unlike. He was short, thin, and pale. I was tall, lanky, and athletic. He was moody, quiet, chain-smoked, and isolated himself most of the time in his back bedroom. I was outgoing, chatty, social, and the thought of smoking nearly made me gag. He expressed his creativity through his watercolors and I through music. His was interior and deeply personal. Mine was external and showy.

If our differences weren't already substantial, they became even more so when, at eight years of age, he was diagnosed with Type I Diabetes. For the rest of his life, he self-administered insulin twice a day. His energy levels fluctuated so much that participating in athletics was a complicated option for him. At a birthday party, he couldn't eat what the other kids were eating, so even then he stood out as different and odd. And to add to his already restricted life, he could never be too far from the refrigerator where he kept his insulin. It was as if he were forever tethered to an invisible master who refused him a normal and full life. And as the years passed and he became increasingly moody and sullen, our alienation became more strident. He gravitated to friends much like himself, most of whom I didn't like, and no one talked about it.

But there was one hopeful period in our youth when I thought our relationship might take a turn for the better. Our stepfather found an abandoned Model A sitting in the middle of a pasture not far from our house and decided it would be the perfect project for his two teenage sons to tackle together. Being an optimist, full of hope for his two sons, Dad paid the owner an undisclosed sum and, that day, towed it home on the end of a chain he had borrowed from a neighbor. He gave us the use of the garage with the caveat that we had one year to put it into driving condition.

For the next year, my brother and I spent nearly every evening after dinner, after homework, after chores, and after my piano practicing tearing apart that scrap of junk. And we fought and argued every step of the way. In the end, the whole enterprise did nothing to encourage our bonding. If anything, it drove an even wider wedge between us. And when it was street-worthy, Gaylord took *de facto* ownership of that 1930 Model A Ford and rarely allowed me to drive it. I didn't argue my case. It didn't seem worth the effort.

It wasn't until years later after our father died, after Gaylord's first failed marriage, after his diabetes had caused blindness, after I had returned from a year of hitchhiking around Europe, northern Africa, and numerous countries in between, and during my last year of college, that we began to find some middle ground where we could at least share a civil conversation. I'm not certain what turned the tide. Maybe there is a shelf life on animosities and ours simply wore out. Maybe we sensed that time was limited and we longed for a normal brother-to-brother friendship. Whatever the reasons, for the next several years, until his death, we made some cautious but intentional movement towards friendship.

In the fall of 1972, while living in California and halfway through the first year of a Ph.D. program, I received a call from my mother telling me that my brother had died. She didn't know the details and, knowing my mother, most likely didn't want to know them. But apparently there had been a series of events that piled too high for Gaylord to surmount. He was not a resilient person. Within the span of one month, his seeing-eye dog had darted from his side, run into the street, and been killed, his second wife had left their troubled marriage, his job at a local crisis clinic was riffed for lack of funds, and he was beginning to experience further physical and neurological damage from all the years of mismanaging his disease. One day he checked into a local hotel and stopped taking his insulin. Five days later he died alone. He simply gave up. I like to imagine that his last hours were peaceful ones.

I flew to Spokane to conduct his funeral and give the eulogy. My mother's and sister's grief was palpable. My own grief was complicated. How could I grieve for a brother I was only beginning to understand?

Even years later, I sometimes wonder what my parents thought about having two sons who could barely stand to be in the same room together. Did they sense their own failure? Did they ever discuss their sadness for their sons' estrangement? My heart is never at peace when I think about my brother.

I remember a particular day when my two youngest sons were acting out some bitterness and retaliation over a perceived wrongdoing. I'd never spoken about my brother to them before. It was then I told them what a gaping hole had been left in my heart over the squandered relationship with my own brother. I told them that that was a pain they didn't want to bear.

"Trust me," I said, "you don't want to feel the way I feel for the rest of your lives."

They stopped their bickering and stared at me in a kind of sad silence. I think that moment of transparency into my personal pain took us all by surprise.

I'd like to say I miss my brother. But it's hard to miss someone you never really knew. To this day, I regret I didn't try harder.

17

MULES ON THE TRAIL

When I popped my head out of the tent around 6:30 a.m. on the Day Eighteen, I was greeted with another beautiful, cloudless morning. I had pitched my tent about twenty feet from the lake so I could hear the gentle lapping of the water on the sandy beach. I think I could have lain there all morning just listening. I decided that day to make no plans for mileage or goals where I would stop and make camp. I would hike at whatever pace felt comfortable and let the day come as it might. I figured I would get a few miles past Chinook Pass, but that was all the planning I was willing to do.

I was on the trail a little after 7:00 a.m., headed for Dewey Lake some five miles north. About two miles into the morning, I came upon a Youth Conservation Crew doing some maintenance on the trail. What they were doing seemed nonessential, but they all seemed happily busy and working well together. I stopped for a few minutes to ask about their group and thank them for their hard work and commitment to improving the trail. I also mentioned that if they really wanted to be helpful to hikers, they could encourage the "powers that be" to place better signage along the Trail. The leader of the group responded that it was a comment he had heard from several other hikers over the past several days. I doubted any action would be taken about the signage, but at least he received another hiker's input. As I left the group and walked a path that circled a large meadow the size of two football fields, I could see in the distance several tents where they had made camp for their week of trail maintenance.

A couple miles farther, I reached Dewey Lake, which was probably the largest lake I had seen thus far. At ten in the morning, there was no one in sight. I located a flat, sandy spot along the shore where I could strip down, jump into the cold water with a bar of soap, and take a quick, much-welcome bath. For the second time since leaving the Columbia Gorge, I unabashedly swam naked. I figured if anyone was near enough to see me in my pure nudity, they would either have to celebrate their good fortune or simply turn away. There was nothing that was going to keep me from enjoying an early morning bathing experience and a few minutes basking on a sunny rock by the shore. Sometimes, a guy just has to take a few risks. It was worth every moment.

After about an hour of this bliss, I got dressed and got back on the trail, feeling wonderfully refreshed. I don't think it helped me hike any faster, but I sure felt better at the pace I was maintaining. I even shaved that morning (with cold lake water!), which perked me up even more. The sky was bright blue, a well-marked trail followed along the lake, and the only sound was my own footsteps. Several meadows were blooming in wildflowers, and I had the morning to myself. So far it had been a very good day.

Soon the trail headed northward away from Dewey Lake towards a series of switchbacks. As I hiked upwards to higher elevations, I could look back and see the entire lake in all its pristine blue beauty. Off in the distance, I spotted a tent that looked about the size of something I'd use as a marker in a Monopoly game. It was the only sign of campers anywhere around the lake. After nearly an hour of steep switchback hiking, I lost sight of Dewey Lake.

Around noon, a few day hikers from Chinook Pass passed me on their way to the lake. Some were carrying a daypack while others had nothing but water bottles strapped to their hips. The weather was perfect. It was a good day to hike for all of us. But I was headed for Chinook Pass about five miles away and as far north from there as my energy would take me for the day. I calculated that I was about a day ahead of where I had figured I would be at this juncture of my hike, so I was in no need to step up my pace or worry about taking too much time to chat with folks along the trail. I was just a little hungry for simple conversation with people who all looked so clean and fresh! From some of the women, I got a scent of perfume and then I REALLY missed Carla!

I crossed the bridge over Highway 410 around 2:00 p.m. and found a spot along the outer perimeter of the parking lot to eat some lunch. There were about thirty cars and RVs parked in the lot. Chinook Pass was a popular starting point for day hikers going north or south.

Several trucks pulled into the parking lot while I sat eating my typical lunch of trail mix, jerky, and a candy bar. One of the trucks was emitting some pretty awful stuff from its tailpipe, giving me a headache, so I cut short my lunch break, packed up my foodstuffs, and headed out of the lot. Good riddance, I thought as I walked the perimeter of the lot in search of the trailhead.

Once back on the trail, I was again confronted by a steep climb. The temperature had risen to around ninety degrees, so I wasn't hiking a very fast pace. I had plenty of water and took several breaks over the next few miles to enjoy the scenery and take a few swigs of water.

Two women passed me going towards the Pass to their car and offered me a few candy bars and granola bars they hadn't needed for their day hike. I gratefully accepted and kept heading northward. I believe something almost cellular happens to people when they get away from their typical, daily routines of work and various other responsibilities and go into the wilderness. We become more trusting and generous, we seem to be more open to expressing joy, and we seem willing to do with less. Often we claim the need for more experiences into the wilds. We even make promises to ourselves that such will be the case. Yet we rarely follow through. When we do, I think we are usually better for it.

The day was the hottest yet. My feet were killing me, and I was weary from yesterday's long mileage. All sounded like solid excuses to cut the day short and camp by a small but idyllic lake five miles north of Chinook Pass. The choice was camping here (the second Sheep Lake on the Trail) or heading several miles up a steep grade to Sourdough Pass and northward into an area where I was uncertain about the availability of water. It was about 4:00 p.m., so it seemed reasonable to end the day by the shore of the lake.

I had been sitting against a tree for about an hour, partly dozing and partly daydreaming, when I heard the sounds of hoofs and the rattling of something I couldn't detect. When I sat up and looked southward from where I had come just an hour earlier, I could see two men on horses, each leading mules behind them. As they came closer, I could make out an older man with a younger man trailing a few feet behind. The two mules were laden with packer's boxes, and both men had sheathed rifles attached to their horses' sides. They looked like something out of a Hollywood western: two trappers on their way to higher ground for wild game—*Jeremiah Johnson* came to mind. As they rode closer, the older of the two yelled out to me, "Howdy, young feller! Mind if me and my grandson park ourselves out there in yonder meadow?" I swear I shook my head, thinking they had time-traveled out of the nineteenth century.

But they were for real. I responded, still with surprise written over my face, "Okay by me. Lots of room around here."

"You camped here for the day?" he asked, while firmly gripping the reins of his horse that seemed ready to bolt at any second.

"Yeah, I came up from Anderson Lake this morning. Too damned hot for more hiking, so I'm just hanging around for the rest the day. Go'n to head for Sourdough Pass tomorrow morning when it's cooler."

"That's our thought. No water for several miles."

"Good look'n animals you got there," I said just to keep things friendly.

"Thanks. We unloaded back at the Pass, and my wife's go'n to meet up with us at Snoqualmie Pass next week."

I just stood smiling at the whole scene.

"We're gonna head on over to that meadow so the animals can graze. C'mon over this evening for a cigar and some whiskey." His grip on the reins remained tight. "You *do* like cigars and whiskey, don't you?"

"I've been known to. Yeah, I'll make my way over this evening. Thanks."

The boy hadn't said a word, but sat tall on his horse while attentively watching his grandfather. They rode off on the path that circled the lake and, after about two hundred yards, cut over towards the lush, green meadow about a quarter mile in the distance.

The grandfather, Hank, was a rancher from Spokane, and Robbie was his grandson. Hank had been horse-camping in the Cascades since he was a young boy, when his own grandfather had taken him out on long rides to hunt and fish or repair trails from the damage of winter storms.

When I reached their camping area in early evening, after I had finished dinner and cleaned up, there was a roaring fire, and both Hank and Robbie were comfortable in their respective camping chairs. Robbie was sipping a soda and Hank was puffing on a cigar and sipping bourbon out of a tin cup. They both appeared delighted that I had taken them up on their offer to join them. After Hank found me a comfortable place to sit by the fire, he offered me a cigar and a cup to pour some whiskey in. I accepted the first and took a pass on the second. What I really wanted was the bourbon and a pass on the cigar. I figured I should at least accept half of Hank's hospitality.

***

There was a time when I would have accepted both the cigar *and* the whiskey. There was a time when I would have brought my own whiskey and most likely drunk the entire bottle the first night on the trail. Alcohol has been trouble for me since I took my first drink at age fourteen. The sensation was so profound and startling that I clearly remember it almost six decades later. It was as if my entire body had shouted out, "Thank you, Jesus, for this most wonderful feeling of empowerment and comfort!" I didn't start drinking again until I was well beyond college and into graduate school, but when I began again, I drank with a vengeance. It was as if I had never stopped. That's why alcoholism is called a "progressive disease," because it progresses as if the person drinking never took a break of any duration.

My history of drinking has been nothing less than disastrous. I usually considered myself in control and believed that a half bottle of scotch or two bottles of wine gave me a clearer sense of well-being. But in fact, it made me stupid and irresponsible and an unbearable douchebag. With profound awareness and regret, I acknowledge I've polluted the lives of anyone who got too close. I was the last person to realize it, even though I was drinking myself into an early grave. Unfortunately, in the more important things in life, I have been a slow learner. It wasn't until I had nearly lost everything—health, family, self-respect, profession, home, and finances—that I finally and begrudgingly sought treatment. And even then I fought sobriety as if it were the enemy out to spoil my life by depriving me of what I most loved. Over the course of several years, I have made earnest and sincere attempts to clean up the wreckage my drinking life wrought, but even so, some damage can never be mended.

My biological father chose booze over his family, and I didn't want his legacy to ruin mine, though I sometimes feared his blood was running through my own veins. I had spent most of my life attempting to be comfortable in my own skin yet being afraid so much of the time. That's what the women and degrees and booze were about. But in the end, I understand it had little to do with my alcoholic, biological father.

Libraries are filled with books, articles, and research about the scourge of alcohol and the devastation it has visited upon countless millions of individuals, families, and communities. While this is not the forum to recount my own litany of disasters and failures, suffice it to say that alcohol has never been my friend. Had it not been for the mercy and tough love of Carla, it's a safe bet that I would not have lived to this point in my life. There was a poignant moment during my early sobriety when I understood with absolute clarity that, over the course of my drinking life, whenever I was up to my eyeballs in shit, alcohol was always a factor. I knew I wouldn't be hiking on the PCT were I not sober. I also knew that, while I didn't choose to be an alcoholic, I could choose to be sober.

Did I want to sit by the campfire with Hank and sip a cup of bourbon? Damned straight I did, but not at the cost it would have extracted. So I puffed on a cigar with gratitude that I was sitting by the campfire with these two generous new acquaintances.

***

There was no moon, so the stars were especially bright. In the spaces of silence between us, I could hear the animals clanging around with their hobbled feet in the distant meadow. Hank offered me another cigar, but the first had left me slightly dizzy, so I declined and told them I needed an early start to beat the heat up to the Pass. They were also headed in that direction, and we agreed to meet up in the next day or two.

Early into our conversation, my antennae picked up that Hank was, in no uncertain terms, against the possibility that Obama might be the next President, so I intentionally kept a wide clearance from any conversation that seemed to veer in that direction. Instead we talked about farming and horses and hunting. I complimented him on being a remarkable grandfather who took time to teach his grandson how to be self-reliant and gain a respect for the out-of-doors. The last thing I said to Hank before I departed for the night was that if all the grandfathers in the world did for their grandchildren what he was doing for Robbie, the world would be a far better place for us all. I could see that comment pleased him and Robbie alike. I made my way across the meadow back to my campsite.

Before I climbed into my tent, I put away the large hunk of homemade bread and a second cigar Hank had given me. Now in my tent, I took out my journal and wrote about the encounter with two open and generous cowboys I had met that day.

Journal Entry:

A reflection about people who come to the wilderness: Once here, we almost become transformed into the people we have always wanted to be but, for some reason or another, have been afraid to take that step towards trust and generosity. I wonder what it is that gets in the way.

Being in the presence of Hank and Robbie, I can't stop thinking about how my own children's grandfather has been so absent in their lives. He has missed an opportunity for great friendship and fun and memories with amazing kids.

18

A BASIN FULL OF ELK

I awoke to the sound of the distant, hobbled horses and mules. Hank hung bells them so no matter how far they might stray during the night, he could locate them as they ate their way around the lush meadow. I could hear them, and it made me smile.

I lay in my warm sleeping bag around 6:00 a.m. on Day Nineteen, but I wanted to beat the heat of the day so I coaxed myself out of the tent and lit my stove for an early morning cup of instant coffee. I sat on a nearby rock and looked down at the lake, thinking how fortunate I had been with all the perfect days I had experienced thus far. This morning was no exception: the crisp morning air, the smell of a dewy meadow, the sky so blue it looked almost unnatural. Absent were of all the noises of phones, traffic, radios, and idle conversations. And today no one would flip me off because I wasn't driving ten miles over the speed limit. This was bliss.

Despite an early start, the morning was hot and dusty, though I managed to reach Sourdough Gap at 6,440 feet before the sun got too high in the sky. The two-mile hike from Sheep Lake to the gap was a seven-hundred-foot rise in elevation. But once I reached the top, the views were magnificent. From my perch, I could see for miles around the rugged beauty of the William O. Douglas Wilderness, south to the path I had already traversed and north to the trail I would hike for the next couple of days. With endless spaciousness, I could see for untold miles in the distance— rock formations, lakes, streams, a bright blue sky contrasting the green and brown landscape. It was a beautiful sight. I sat on a rock that jutted out over the edge, chewed on a piece of turkey jerky, and took a few minutes to catch my breath. I stared down at Sheep Lake and the adjoining meadows, where I had camped last night, and credited myself for possessing the good sense to stop early yesterday, take advantage of a perfect camping area, and enjoy the unexpected pleasure of an evening with Hank and Robbie. They were on their way to Snoqualmie Pass, so I calculated I'd see them again somewhere along the trail. They would have to make camp where there was grazing and fresh water for the stock. I'd only have to listen for the bells to find them again.

From Sourdough Gap, I spent the rest of the day hiking a trail that offered up views of Mt. Rainier, Bear Gap, Crystal Mountain Ski Area, Pickhandle Point, and Crown Point, arriving finally at Scout Pass, where the trail brought me along a ridge above Basin Lake. From there it was a fairly steep drop into the basin, which meant I would have a steep climb back out tomorrow. Throughout most of the day, I had hiked in open country, so the heat had taken its toll. There had been a few places where pine trees had provided a welcomed canopy, but otherwise the sun beat down on me. And I was minus my trusty red cap.

Around noon I came to a ridge where it seemed I could almost reach out and touch the side of Mt. Rainer. Its beauty was almost staggering. I found a comfortable rock where I could sit, eat a quick lunch, and stare at the magnificent, snowy wonder. I had been sitting for less than a minute when I heard the sounds of other hikers coming up the trail towards where I sat. As the two young men approached, I recognized them from an encounter several days earlier along the trail.

"You again!" one of them said.

"Yeah, I'm slow, but I just keep popping up from place to place."

They stopped and stood a few feet across from me, blocking my view of the mountain.

"Taking a lunch break?" one of them asked.

"More like a view break."

"What?"

"Mt. Rainer. I'm just sitting here to stare at it."

One of them turned around.

"Oh shit! I didn't even notice it."

"How the hell can you not notice the biggest fucking mountain in the state?" I chimed in with a chuckle.

"I just get so wrapped up in hiking, I sometimes forget to see what's in front of me."

"Well, it took me my entire life to get to this very spot where I'm sitting, so I'm going to take advantage of it. Likely, I'll never be at this place again."

It often happened that thru hikers wouldn't notice the scenery. They were focused on hiking the monster miles and gauged their progress by mileage rather than places. I sat for a few more minutes after they headed up the trail. I was in no rush, and it was a fact of my life that I would never be at this place again. I wanted to take full advantage of my unobstructed view.

Though most days I would have hiked another three or four hours, at 3:00 p.m. my maps didn't show another definite close source of water once I left the Basin Lake area. I decided to cut the day short and head down towards the lake. The Scout Pass trail was about 6,600 feet and the lake was at 5,800 feet, so the half-mile hike into the basin to the lake was a steep drop over an ill-defined trail and loose rocks. As I came closer to the lake, I heard the sound of water on its way down the steep pathway towards the lake. In about fifty yards, the shallow brook crossed the trail. I stopped and sat on the grassy ground next to the brook and poured cold water over my face and head then filled my water bottles, even though I was only a few yards from the lake. I simply liked the idea of fresh, running water. I looked up at the pass from where I had just come down and took a mental note that I would have one hell of a climb in the morning. But at least it would be in the cool of the morning, and I would be rested.

I reached Basin Lake around 3:30 p.m. There was no one in sight. I had the lake and all the surrounding camping areas to myself. It wasn't a very large lake, maybe thirty acres, and was fed by several small streams coming down off the adjacent mountains. The surrounding area was flat with several clumps of trees that served as camping areas. It looked to be a place where horse campers might set up camp during hunting season. There were traces that animals had come and gone and, unfortunately, traces of campers who hadn't gotten the memo to "leave no trace." Right there in the midst of all the beauty of water and greenery were messes left by former campers. I stood looking around, feeling pretty pissed off. Moreover, the area had been picked clean of firewood, so I abandoned the idea of a campfire for the night. It was still pretty warm and it seemed the evening would also be warm, so I even considered not pitching my tent. But then, there was something reassuring about having that small space where I was zipped up and private.

Around the time I sat down on a nearby log for dinner, the bugs arrived. They weren't after my dinner. They were after me! So I quickly finished the remainder of my beef stew, set up my tent, and dove in for protection from the pesky gnats. As I sat inside the protective barrier and ate a candy bar, I watched the bugs dive at the fabric as if they could penetrate in and get at me. Ha, I was safe from harm, so I lay on my sleeping bag and listened to angry bugs dive-bombing my tent.

Just before nightfall, the noise from the bugs abated, and I took the risk of venturing out. The bugs had either abandoned their fruitless attacks or had, themselves, headed home. I had pitched my tent about fifteen yards from the lake, so walked to the shore and sat watching several trout jumping with hopes of snagging a pesky bug flying close to the water. I was rooting for the trout.

The sun was making its descent behind the nearest peak. Since I was camped in a deep basin, the light of the day dimmed quicker than usual. So I called it a good day and headed back to the tent. After such an arduous and hot day of difficult trails, I could use the extra sleep.

Safely in my tent and tucked into my sleeping bag, I wrote in my journal for the next several minutes, then switched off my headlight, said my usual nightly prayer of thanks, and settled in. I needed to be up earlier than usual to accomplish more miles than a typical day. Carla was expecting me to reach Snoqualmie Pass by Sunday, and I didn't want to worry her if I wasn't on schedule. There would be a reload box waiting for me, and I planned to get a room at the motel and take a zero day with several showers and a load of laundry. I was also hoping to catch up with Hank and Robbie before they headed home.

Journal Entry
I took lots of water and view breaks today. Not too much mileage, but there is beauty in the sheer effort, no matter how far or how quickly I have hiked.

***

Day Twenty was a Friday, and I awoke earlier than planned with little sleep from the previous night. I was already cranky before I'd even started the day. My intentions for an early-to-bed good night's sleep had been thwarted by a herd of elk that had come into camp around two in the morning and made such loud grunting and rooting noises that I hardly slept a solid hour for the rest of the night. A couple times I got out of the tent, found one of my pots, and banged it against my cup, blew my whistle, and shouted into the dark for all of them to shut the hell up. It worked for a few minutes, but they quickly returned to their noisy grazing and grunting. It was disarming to think of enormous, horned animals a few feet from where I was lying, realizing full well that the thin fabric of my tent would provide no armor from any one of them if it decided to stampede in the direction of my silly pot-banging and commands for silence. After all, I thought, I needed the sleep far more than they needed their midnight snacks. Finally, I begrudgingly got up to start the day. I figured it would be about an hour climb back to Scout Pass and the trail headed towards Government Meadow about fifteen miles north in the Norse Peak Wilderness.

It seemed odd that even after all that noise from last night's herd of elk, there didn't appear to be one sign of their ever being there. They arrived, uttered annoying noises, grazed most of the night, and left without a trace. Spooky.

I finished my one cup of coffee, wrote a few paragraphs in my journal, slung The Rock on my back, and headed out of the basin. It was a beautiful, idyllic spot, and another one of those unplanned places that gave me pause for gratitude and for the beauty and wonder of what I was experiencing.

As it turned out, the climb out of the basin wasn't as difficult as I had thought. It took only a half hour to get back to the trail.

19

TURNABOUT TIME

As I stood next to the path looking at my map to be certain I was headed in the right direction, I saw the figure of a hiker approaching. His gait was crooked and measured, and it appeared he was favoring a leg or foot. As he came closer, I saw that his knee was crudely bandaged, his pack looked enormous, and he was limping. This man, who looked to be in his mid-forties, was a sorry sight for me to behold only one hour into the day.

Rich had started his hike at White Pass several days prior. The previous day he'd taken a pretty hard fall off a boulder he was hiking over. I remembered the area from my own experience and knew about where he had fallen. Given the terrain, tripping and falling would have been an easy thing to do. Along with a twisted ankle, he had opened up a pretty nasty gash on his left kneecap. But even with his injuries, he was determined to make it to Snoqualmie Pass to meet his wife and head home to Oregon. I had serious doubts whether he would be able to hike the demanding sixty miles to his destination. I kept my thoughts about his condition to myself, along with my opinion that his decision to continue wasn't a wise one. His pack appeared far too heavy, and he was packing a few extra pounds around his midsection. Rich was the first person I had encountered on the trail who actually was "overweight." Most hikers were thin, muscular, with minimal body fat. But out of sheer determination and guts, Rich wasn't about to abandon his goal—pain, injury, or weight notwithstanding. So we agreed to hike together for a while and see if our paces worked for one another. Just a few days back on the trail, I myself had been rescued by a Trail Angel as I stood by a snowfield, in a state of desperation, pondering my options about continuing or turning back. I figured hanging back for a little while with

Rich would be a minor cosmic payback, and besides, I was ready for some companionship.

We quickly agreed that Rich would take the lead and set the pace. Watching him hobble along with that bummed ankle and gashed knee was a painful thing to witness. I walked about twenty feet behind, but he was a tough bird and kept a pretty decent pace and a good attitude. We chatted as we hiked. Rich was a geography teacher at a small Oregon community college, and hiking the PCT was a challenge he had wanted to attempt for several years. In his own words, he wasn't getting any younger or lighter, so he figured this was the year. Like Carla, Rich's wife had told him to either do it or shut the hell up about it.

After a few miles of covering the basics in conversation—Where you from? What do you do? How long you been married? Any kids? Etc.—we got to talking a little about politics. As it turned out, he and I were pretty similar in our views. Then came an interesting moment. We were taking a short water break after about three miles and giving his knee a few minutes respite when he asked me if I had heard the latest big political news. I told him I hadn't heard anything about anything since I'd left home almost three weeks prior. And then he asked if I wanted a recap on the political scene. I told him an emphatic "No!" Being the political news wonk that I am, I would usually lap up any news like a thirsty dog, but while on the PCT, I was satisfied with ignorance. Not only did I not miss all the political rhetoric that was choking the airways with hostility and bullshit, there was little else I missed or craved. I had everything I needed or wanted right on my back, and aside from conversations with my wife, I lacked for nothing.

But Rich pressed on. "Then can I just say two words?" he pleaded.

"Two words and that's it," I responded.

"Yeah, well, that's all you'll need to hear."

"Okay, but I don't want a recap."

Rich paused, looked at me with a wide grin, and said, "Paul Ryan."

I immediately burst into laughter, jumped up, and did my happy dance. "Holy Christ, Mitt just shot himself in the foot!" I was gleeful beyond description. "Shit, they just lost the election."

"I hope you're right. But those sonsabitches have more money than God to push any agenda."

"All the fucking money in the world won't get Mitt elected with that self-righteous prick as his running mate."

I was feeling pretty cocky and self-assured about that fact. It truly was the only political news I had heard in weeks. And that was all I needed to hear. The rest was just working out the kinks and waiting for the first week of November.

About two hours into the morning, I heard the sound of hoofs coming up behind us. It was Hank and Robbie. They had camped last night about a half mile north of Basin Lake, where I had camped, and were expecting me to show up, bedraggled and hungry. Both seemed genuinely disappointed, but encouraged me to forge on and meet them at Urich Camp next to Government Meadows. Without even knowing exactly where that lay in the scheme of my day, I agreed.

I had stepped off the trail to let them pass, and as Robbie came alongside of me, he was holding a shirt I had slipped under a strap on the top of my pack to dry out from perspiration. Clearly I hadn't secured it tightly enough and a low-hanging branch had probably snagged it as I passed by. I think Robbie wanted to keep it for himself, but since he was about three sizes larger than me, it wasn't difficult to convince him to give it up. Robbie even offered to walk for a while and let me ride his horse. I declined his sincere offer with a burst of laughter. I think Rich was a little worried that he might lose his newly found hiking partner if I accepted Robbie's offer. But there was no way I was going to abandon Rich, and no way was I going to get on a horse I didn't know. It's risky business riding strange horses. I preferred the safety of my feet on the ground.

"Thanks, Robbie, but that'd be cheating," I said looking up at him and grinning.

Robbie just smiled down on me and clicked his tongue, gave the horse's flank a gentle kick, and headed up the trail.

***

It is a rarity to be totally unplugged from all the layers upon layers of the noise and clamor of every manmade device that vies for our attention: TV, radio, computers, iPods, cell phones, billboards, idle conversations in the lunch room, *ad nauseam.* To be in the wilderness without distractions is a blessed thing. To be sure, there are noises in the wilderness: the sound of wind, birds scolding one another for invading their spaces, the water of a stream breaking over rocks, or bees and bugs buzzing overhead. But those sounds are natural and holy. To have been absent from the babble of the political rhetoric was pure relief. All the sound bites from political wonks and talking heads were not going to sway the direction of the impending elections, and once I got a strong hold on that fact, I was relieved to be absent from it all. My heart was calmer, my head less muddled, and my soul less conflicted. Mostly, I felt less angry. But those two words from Rich—Paul Ryan—lifted my spirits. I sort of floated over the trail for the next several miles. Then reality struck. I was still carrying a heavy pack, my feet hurt, it was a hot day, and I had another ten miles of hard hiking to reach where I planned to camp for the night.

***

"Hey, there's a rib-eye steak in the cooler with your name on it!" Hank yelled out.

I had barely caught sight of him and Robbie, but they could see me making my way up the trail towards their campsite at Urich Camp along Government Meadows. They were about two hours ahead of me and had already set up their tents, camp tables, and chairs, had a fire lit, and were preparing dinner. They'd figured I'd be along before dark, so decided to wait for my arrival. It was another great surprise, and I welcomed "real" food for the dinner meal.

Rich had developed some pretty nasty blisters and lagged about an hour behind me. I wanted to stay with him, but he wasn't even certain he would hike any farther. I left him sitting on a log with his boots and socks removed, showing just how beat up his feet were. They were a pretty ghastly sight. He had so overcompensated his stride because of his twisted ankle and damaged knee that blisters had formed in seemingly impossible places. I sat with him for a few minutes, trying to console him and encourage him to get off his feet for the day and make camp right there off the trail. But he was pretty determined to get in a few extra miles before nightfall. I left him with most of my Band-Aids and some surgical tape before I continued on to Urich Camp about four miles north of where we sat.

According to my map, Government Meadows was a thirty-acre meadow that, during the winter months, was an area used by snowboarders. I figured Hank might have his horses and mules hobbled there for an overnight of grazing.

The steak was from a steer Hank had butchered from his own herd just a few months prior. I believe it was the best piece of meat I had ever devoured. And as we three sat around the campfire, sharing that sumptuous meal, the conversation soon turned to the state of the nation. I did my level best to keep the conversation simple: past backpacking experiences, biggest fish I ever caught, "the good ol' days," what's wrong with kids today, and horses in our pasts we loved and hated. The fire felt good and the company even better, and I felt a tinge of guilt about leaving Rich behind, but he was pretty adamant that he wanted to rest and reconsider whether or not to continue for the day. Still, I wished he could be around the fire sharing all this goodness.

That night, I stayed up longer than any other night since I'd begun. There's something mystical and comforting about sitting around a campfire sharing stories. There are really very few places and times where that can occur in today's culture. But there we were, three strangers:

a farmer from eastern Washington who takes his grandchildren on packing trips into the mountains and is as right-wing a person as I've spoken with since I can remember, a seventeen-year-old grandson about the size of my truck but gentle and respectful with an understanding of how rare and fortunate an experience he was having with his grandfather, and me, a senior citizen hiking alone a long way from home and a long way from anything remotely in common with the other two men sharing that campfire. It was nearly midnight when we decided we had talked just about enough for one day and left the warmth of the fire.

Several years earlier, a snowboarding organization had built a one-story log cabin on the edge of the meadow. So that night I threw my sleeping bag and pad on the wooden floor, latched the door, and settled in for the night. At least there wouldn't be a herd of elk to contend with.

20

LOG HOUSES PAST AND PRESENT

On the morning of Day Twenty-Two, I once again awoke to the sound of hobbled mules and horses clanging their bells as they made their way around the meadow. Unfortunately, the night had not been as peaceful as I'd hoped. I'd missed the memo about the mice. They had taken residence in, under, and around the cabin, and I was most certainly the intruder in their space. I awoke several times to their pattering little feet scurrying about. It would have been a gold mine for the mousetrap industry. I'm sure there were only a handful of the little critters making the entire racket, but it sounded like an invading army. So, once again, I chalked it up to the price of being a guest in the wilderness. Whatever bug or rodent appeared, they had first dibs on the space. Sleep in a log cabin and you get mice. Sleep outside under the stars and you get the sound of hobbled animals, a herd of elk, and a morning dewy tent.

The night was disruptive, but that seemed minor as I started the day in the presence of another beautiful morning. I boiled some water for coffee and sat on the steps of the cabin looking out at the lush green meadow. There was a thin layer of mist that clung to the grassy surface. The animals were about a hundred yards away, and in the silence of the early morning I watched them graze totally unaware of anything or anyone around them. What a peaceful existence, I thought. As I sat on those steps, it was the first time in years I thought about the log house I'd built and the fire that had burned it to ashes.

***

The fire was twenty years ago, but sometimes the memory can burn a searing pain in my heart. I nearly lost my wife and our two sons. We lost everything else, but none of us were so much as singed. And as fortune would have it, our daughter, Paige, was away visiting her grandmother and thus escaped the entire episode. Reflecting on that night, I don't think I could have carried all three children down the stairway and out of the burning house. Two small sons, ages ten months and four years, were armful enough, so I figured I'd won that round.

Years before, I was single, deep into my professional life, living in a beautiful home, and earning a decent salary with a future that promised success and notice. I left it all behind to move to an island in Puget Sound. Philip, my son from my first marriage, was living in California with his mother and her husband. It would be a colossal understatement to say that he was experiencing difficulty with that arrangement. So it was decided that Philip would move to the Northwest where he and I would begin our life together. Because I'm not big on restoring classic cars, I decided that our father-son bonding project would be to build a log house on some raw property I had purchased the previous year.

After the Douglas fir trees were felled and delivered on the property, Philip and I took on the daunting task of debarking them with hand tools and, with an old 1959 crane I rented, we began the long and challenging task of building a log house on those twenty acres. With no electricity, we used hand tools and a temperamental generator, ropes, pulleys, and long days of grunting and sweating. The walls were constructed in about four months. But then the real work began: building the subfloor, installing windows, constructing a roof, configuring the interior walls, and everything else required to make a house habitable. There was a time, about halfway through the process, that I seriously contemplated bringing a few gallons of kerosene to the site and burning it down. But with the encouragement of friends, my higher and more reasonable self prevailed, and the house was ready for occupancy in the fall of 1984.

Now, over thirty years later, I barely remember what the root of my motivation or drive was to move to that island, to leap into the vast series of unknowns, to leave a job without knowing how I would survive, and to raise a son without an income. I had worked at some job or vocation since I was twelve. But quite suddenly, and with minimal fanfare, I cut all ties to what had become familiar and safe. And yet, as I sat and swirled the coffee in my cup and looked out at a peaceful meadow, I knew, given the opportunity, I would do it all over again. Leaving my job, a life in the city, and the comfort of the tried and true, I was happier and more content than I had ever remembered being.

I suppose what best summed up such a radical decision was my personal search for a meaning that was not going to be defined by my work or a paycheck or a better car or finding another elegant restaurant to patronize. And too, within a blink of an eye, I had transformed from a single man with no ties and little accountability to a single father expected home at night to prepare dinner for my son, pack his lunch each morning, do laundry, check homework, attend assorted school meetings, show up while he participated in sports programs, and deal with all the other minutia that accompanied a life of parenting. Nothing would ever be the same. Soon after moving into the house, on a beautiful fall Saturday morning, Philip and I planted a single Gravenstein apple tree. In the ensuing years, I added other fruit trees that grew the orchard to nearly eighty trees.

Eight years later and a week after my fiftieth birthday, Carla, my wife of five years, and I awoke to the horrifying sounds of a crackling fire. On that dark and dreary November morning, Carla and I stood helplessly and watched our home being consumed by flames so immense they could be seen for miles in the distance.

That log house was where I married Carla and where our son, Jonah, was born in our bedroom on the second floor. After the fire, we rebuilt a new home where the log house once stood, but nothing was ever the same, there or in my own heart. A few years later, Carla and I left the new house and the land and moved our family of two sons and a daughter to another place nearby.

That early morning, sitting on the steps of the log cabin adjacent to Government Meadows, I thought mostly of all those trees I'd planted there that, even now, still bearing fruit. I miss that orchard more than I miss the house, yet it was the place where Carla and I began our life together.

I hoped the orchard would be a legacy left for others to enjoy for many years to come.

***

I could hear Hank and Robbie beginning to pack up their gear. And there was a lot to pack up, because with pack mules there's no lack of stuff that can be brought. Heck, Hank and Robbie even had a folding camping table, folding lawn chairs, and two ice coolers filled with great food!

Hank came around the corner and saw me sitting on the steps.

"Looks like you're into some deep thinking."

"Yeah, mulling over some past heartache."

"That's dangerous. Not something I'd recommend doing this early in the day."

"Well, reflection's not for the faint-hearted," I responded.

"So, how 'bout taking your reflecting butt off that stoop and come along with me to catch the animals?"

"As long as they don't spit," I said with a chuckle.

"You're confusing your animals," Hank responded without looking back at me.

It was my attempt at a lame joke. I knew exactly what I was getting into. More times than I enjoy remembering, I'd fetched my own horses in open fields with about fifty-fifty success. But I had never tried to coax a mule into compliance. This would be a first.

I tossed the remainder of the coffee off to one side, set my cup on the step, and jumped to the ground to follow Hank, who was carrying halter ropes and bridle bits for the animals. He looked over his shoulder as he handed me a bucket of oats. The oats would be used to entice the animals to come towards us. It was a familiar routine, but I hadn't attempted to lure an animal in an open field for more than twenty years, let alone get a bit into its mouth. The good thing was that they were hobbled, so couldn't run too fast or far. But still, the mules were large and forbidding, and I wasn't especially excited to put halter ropes around them. I just wanted to grab a quick breakfast and get on the trail, but I figured, for all the generosity Hank had shown me, the least I could do was follow him through the meadow and gather the stock.

Robbie was back at camp cooking breakfast, and I could smell the bacon fifty yards away. I wondered how anything that smelled so good could be so bad for me. My stomach grumbled, and the thought of a dry breakfast bar didn't seem too appealing. I think Robbie was probably grinning while watching me tag along behind his grandfather.

After we had coaxed the animals to come close enough to the oats to get them haltered, we headed back towards where Robbie had breakfast waiting. Hank invited me to stay and share another meal. The offer was far too tempting to reject. The smell of bacon cooking on an open fire was nothing a sane person could walk away from. It was nearly 8:30 a.m. and I needed to get on the trail if I wanted to make it to Tacoma Pass eighteen miles north, but I weakened and opted for a hot breakfast. Of course.

Back on the trail around 9:30 a.m., I was worried about Rich and wondered how he was faring with his bum knee and blistered feet. I hadn't seen him pass me on the trail after I'd stopped last night, so wasn't sure of his whereabouts. Given his gimpy pace, I figured I would see him eventually. I just wasn't certain when or where. For the second time, I said my goodbyes to Hank and Robbie with my heartfelt thanks. I think they were genuinely disappointed I wasn't hanging around for a few more cups of coffee. But, as my new cowboy friends said, I was "burn'n daylight" and I needed to get hiking. Even with the long miles I hoped to hike, I estimated that I would arrive at Snoqualmie Pass a day later than I had thought.

***

On Day Twenty-Two I awoke to a gray morning. It was the first time since I'd left the Columbia Gorge that the morning sky had been anything less than a perfectly clear and deeply blue. The previous night, I had practically fallen into bed from utter exhaustion. It had taken me until midmorning to get on the trail. I was just having too much fun helping Hank corral and hitch up the horses, accepting Robbie's generous offer to share their breakfast, and hanging around to swap a few more stories. I think, had they an extra horse, I might have been tempted to ride to Snoqualmie Pass rather than hike. Fortunately, that temptation wasn't available.

I was sitting with my back against a tree near where I had pitched my tent last night. There was a cup of hot coffee I had placed on a rock next to me. I could have been on the trail an hour ago, but I just wanted to sit and write in my journal before I began the day.

Journal Entry:
Wouldn't mind having a cup of the brewed coffee Robbie made yesterday morning. In comparison, instant crystals just don't cut it.

What a gift to have met Hank and Robbie. I felt like family. I think Hank enjoyed the adult company, and Robbie liked the fact that I paid so much attention to him. I taught him how to sharpen a knife. I think knowing how to sharpen a knife is something every kid should know how to do.

I'm hoping to see them at least one more time before we all arrive at the Pass.

***

The previous day had been a hard day of hiking. I wanted to cover at least fifteen miles, but as it turned out, I hiked nineteen miles in about ten hours. In addition to all the switchbacks, there was a critical lack of water sources. In fact, about two hours before I reached my campsite, I was totally out of water and so damned thirsty I became concerned that I might not have any water until the next day. While my maps and guides indicated there was water along the trail, each time I came to those places, the ponds or streams had dried up. The first couple of times that occurred, I didn't think much about it, but after several hours without reaching a water source, I got a little anxious. And since the morning, I hadn't met anyone along the trail, so couldn't ask about water sources. I had a bad feeling in my gut but kept moving forward, believing I would eventually find something.

By 6:00 p.m., I had been on the trail since early morning and I was completely spent. I had to keep moving in hopes of finding some water. A long-distance hiker has to maintain hope and optimism. The PCT is no place for the faint-hearted or the cynical. I liked to think there was always something good just up the trail and was holding onto that thought when I heard the rushing sounds of a stream in the distance. I dropped The Rock along the trail and headed off in the direction of the sound. But the farther I distanced myself from the trail and my pack, the more disoriented I became. Everything started looking the same and there was nothing—no unique tree or rock or bush— that I could use as a marker for me to find my way back to the trail. I could hear the damned sound of water but couldn't find it, so I turned around after about a half hour of bushwhacking, sans water.

Back on the trail, with my pack feeling even heavier than ever, I headed along with great hope that I would, sooner than later, find the stream I had been hearing over the past hour. I hiked for another two miles, came around a corner, and there sat a young couple beginning the preparations for their evening meal. It was obvious I looked like what the cat had dragged in. They both stood up quickly. Jason helped me get my pack off my back, and Sally gave me one of her water bottles and stood close while watching me chug its entirety with abandon. I hardly took a breath.

"Where the hell am I, and where the hell's the water I keep hearing?" I blurted in between desperate gulps.

"Well, you're about twenty feet from Tacoma Pass, and the water's about twenty feet beyond that," Sally answered calmly. I emptied her water bottle with one last, long swallow and handed it to her.

"Well, give me back your bottle and I'll go fill it along with mine."

"No, you just sit there and rest. I'll take all the bottles and fill them," Jason insisted.

I mildly protested, but he was having none of it. I sat crumpled in a heap of sweat, weariness, and hunger and watched him head down the trail towards the stream. Sally pulled out a large, beautiful, red apple from her pack.

"Here, looks like you could use a piece of fresh fruit."

And there I sat, feeling like a long-lost uncle eating a crisp apple while Sally talked about their own day on the trail.

Jason returned in about fifteen minutes. I had eaten the apple, core and all, and Sally had already helped me set up my tent. Our sites were about twenty feet apart, and we sat together after our respective dinners were cooked. They were hiking to Crystal Mountain about thirty miles south from where we were camped. Sally was a nurse practitioner, and Jason was an engineer. Every summer for the past ten years, they'd taken this same hike from Snoqualmie Pass to Crystal Mountain to celebrate their anniversary.

That day, I had hiked nearly twenty hard miles and was exhausted beyond description, but also elated that I had made up some significant time and might get to Snoqualmie Pass within the next couple days. Every part of my body ached. Clearly I needed at least one zero day to recuperate.

The next morning was cloudy, so I wasn't that keen on getting out of my sleeping bag and starting another long mileage day. Even though I was determined to reach Snoqualmie Pass in the next couple days, I had a difficult time dragging myself out of the tent and getting on the trail. Fortunately, my Irish grit prevailed. I lit my stove to boil some water and used my last couple of packages of the Starbucks coffee crystals Betty had gifted me. From where I sat, I could see the couple pack up and prepare to leave. Sally walked over to where I was sitting up against a tree sipping coffee and gave me another apple with kind words of encouragement. It never ceased to amaze me how many people I had met who showed generosity and concern with no *quid pro quo* expected.

***

Halfway through the morning of Day Twenty-Three, I caught up with Rich. It wasn't difficult. He was in worse shape than the last time I'd seen him, and I doubted even further that he should continue. After several hours of painful hiking, he finally consented, and we made a plan for him to wait along one of the several fire roads we would eventually cross. It was the season for huckleberry picking, so we figured someone would come along and take him down the mountain to Snoqualmie Pass. And so it happened. We parted company in late afternoon and I headed north alone.

I hiked another five miles for a total of ten hours before my feet and back informed me it was time to stop. This was one of those occasions where listening to my body was more important than reaching a mileage goal. But I couldn't locate any place suitable for a campsite. So about an hour before nightfall, I stopped along a level place by the trail, kicked away the stones and dead branches, and set up camp right next to the path. After a quick dinner, I lit a small fire to dry my socks and sweaty shirt while I changed into my thermo clothes. No matter how hot it was in the afternoon, evenings tended to be chilly, especially if I were wet with perspiration. I never wanted to chance getting chilled, so a campfire always felt terrific. Firelight also added a comforting dimension to the camping experience.

Journal Entry:
My socks are steaming from the heat of the fire. I only packed two pairs. One to wear and one for a fresh change

after a couple days. These are my only socks until I get my next reload box. I wear them out, then burn them. They are far beyond ever being clean again!

I don't think it's legal for me to have a fire here, but I don't think any ranger is going to come down the trail and cite me. I'll take the chance. Come to think of it, I have yet to see a ranger on the Trail.

Said my goodbyes to Rich this afternoon at Lizard Lake. I caught up with him about two hours into the morning, and we hiked together for much of the day. His knee and feet were hurting so badly he was practically in tears most of the day. After I convinced him to give up his plans to hike the ten or so miles to Snoqualmie Pass, we stopped along a fire road that looked as though it were pretty well used during this huckleberry season. Sure enough, a fancy-looking SUV came along after we had been sitting by the side of the road for about a half an hour. I waved it down and explained to the driver about Rich needing a ride down the mountain. The car had three passengers, so they declined and drove off. I laughed out loud and told Rich they must not have taken notes during the sermon about, "As you have done this unto the least of these, my brethren, you have done it also unto me." Rich was impressed with my Biblical quotation. He knows nothing about my ministerial background. I never mention it to anyone along the trail.

About fifteen minutes later, the car returned, and they made room for Rich. We hugged and said goodbye. He seemed sad to be leaving. Not sure if it was about me or about leaving the Trail. Maybe some of both. I will miss his company. He gave me his business card, but I've already lost it and I don't know his last name. Rich will remain a fond memory from a few fun days of hiking.

Part of me doesn't want to keep in contact with anyone I've met along the trail. They are good folks, but I am okay just to let our short acquaintance be sufficient for that time. They all have come into my life at just the right moment for all the right reasons, and I am grateful for each one of them. But I have no need to go into the future with them. I think we have been a blessing to one another in some manner or another, and I am satisfied that that is sufficient to stand on its own.

There is no moon, the stars are brilliantly displayed, and my small fire is down to the last embers. Socks and shirt are dry, I am tucked in my sleeping bag and writing by the light of my headlamp. I am beat. If I get a reasonably early start tomorrow, I think I can reach Snoqualmie Pass by late afternoon. Might even cross paths with Hank and Robbie before they head home.

21

THE SIMPLICITY OF DAYS

To arrive at the destination where my reload box was waiting was a near equivalent to Christmas morning. At those places I would often meet up with another PCT hiker taking one or more zero days or even those who had left the trail for several days while attending business back home. And then there were the town residents, often a bit curious why anyone with a shred of sanity would hike several hundreds of miles, sleep on the cold, unforgiving ground, eat crappy food, and leave themselves vulnerable to unpredictable weather and pesky or aggressive animals.

"How the hell do you hike hundreds of miles alone?" was a common question.

"Simple," was my usual response. "I just get up every morning, eat breakfast, pack my gear, put on my boots, strap on my pack, and start walking. Usually in that order."

"I could never do that!"

"Sure you could. You simply decide to do it, and if you're in a reasonable state of good health and have a sliver of discipline, you can make it happen. Maybe not the entire PCT, but a few miles of it. Life doesn't have to be an either-or proposition."

"I don't think I could handle so much quiet and solitude."

"Well, then, that's the rub. Because if you can't do solitude, you can't do the miles. They pretty much go hand in hand. You've got to make peace with boredom. Or, better yet, turn the boredom into something positive."

"Like what?"

"Like reflecting about where you've been in your life. Think about your family and what might be different when you return home. Like having a conversation with yourself about what you're doing with your life and what plans you have for the rest of it."

"You really do all that?"

"Well, it's a hell of a lot better than thinking about the political mess or spending energy being pissed at the traffic or worrying about what could go wrong on any given day."

That was a *verbatim* conversation I had on several occasions with someone impressed with the whole concept of solo hiking. My responses were simply to let my opinion be known about how people tend to complicate very simple things. Life on the trail *was* simple. And I loved its simplicity. It was also routine, though routine doesn't guarantee simplicity. But, for me, there was a certain comfort in the routine of each day. Hiking the PCT was a series of simple day-to-day choices and tasks that only required me to emerge from a cozy sleeping bag every morning and begin the day. How quick my pace or amount of miles covered in a day or the number of water or snack breaks was the choice I made entirely on my own. Unless a hiker was with a group hell-bent to hike a definite number of miles every day, each was accountable only to himself. I met some of those groups (and individuals) who possessed a rigid determination to hike twenty-five to forty miles a day, and there wasn't a lot of downtime between the beginning of the day and its end.

That wasn't my intent. Except on rare occasions, I hiked a simple day of two-miles-per-hour pace, took several breaks to rest, take pictures, or simply sit on a rock or log to look out at a distant mountain or down into a valley where a river flowed.

I was rarely afraid I would get lost or take a spur trail and head off in a wrong direction. However, from time to time, I *was* "in a circle of confusion," solved either by clearer map reading or someone coming up or down the trail and assuring me I was heading in the right direction. And there were times when that did happen. If ever I felt a little too uncertain about my status, I could simply find a comfortable place along the trail, remove The Rock, and wait for someone to come along. That happened on several occasions, but I never had to wait more than a half hour.

Asking for help was never a sign of defeat or an indication of carelessness. I understand men's aversion towards admitting we might possibly not know everything about everything. But for me to ask for assurances that I was heading the right direction was a matter of common sense, not a failure. Given a worst-case scenario, I typically had several days' worth of food, a tent, a stove, and warm clothing. I could wait it out for about a week. That had yet to happen. As it turns out, waiting is often a pleasant pastime that usually turns into a nice moment of chatting, comparing equipment, sharing food, and exchanging encouragements. It was often a time I could jot some thoughts in my journal. Something positive would always come from my sitting and waiting. I had not come all this way to get lost. I could be in a circle of confusion but never lost. It was a simple and uncomplicated manner of living each day on the Trail.

22

HALFWAY THERE

Around 5:00 p.m. on Day Twenty-Four, I reached Snoqualmie Pass. The day had begun at 6:00 a.m. I'd hiked about fifteen miles. It was a lot harder day of hiking than I'd figured it would be, so I decided to take two zero days at the Pass. Aside from the needed rest, I also needed to discuss my backpack problem with someone at REI. I looked forward to the downtime.

The night before was the first time on the trail I hadn't pitched my tent, "cowboy camping" instead, which simply means sleeping on a groundcover under the open sky. Actually, I'd met several PCT hikers who didn't even bring a tent and chose to sleep in the open every night unless there was threat of rain. Then, and only then, they would set up a tarp. But no tent. Those folks were "minimalists" who claimed a tent was too much weight, hard-core hikers who were rigid about keeping their packs around twenty pounds. My tent weighed about two pounds, so for those few extra pounds, I opted for the advantages of tenting. But not last night. Last night the stars were magnificent. During the night, when I awoke to some strange noise, I looked up to witness shooting stars and orbs so bright I could have had ample light to read.

The next morning I awoke to a bright, clear sky. I lay still in the comfortable, warm spot that I had cleared for my sleeping pad and bag. I had slept well and felt full of hope and wondered why I had spent so much of my life stressed and ungrateful.

About three hours into the day, I reached Mirror Lake and met a man who had camped there the previous night. He was packed and ready to start the day, sitting on a log, looking out at the lake with his back to me. I made sufficient noises as I approached him so he wouldn't be startled.

"Getting a late start?" I asked a few feet from where he sat.

He turned around as I approached. "I'm in no hurry. Enjoying the beauty of the morning."

"I've been hiking since first light, so if you don't mind the company, I think I'll sit awhile and rest before my last leg to the Pass."

"Plenty of rocks here for sitting."

We sat together for a half hour. Sam looked to be in his early fifties. He had recently retired from a job in airline security and was taking some personal time to figure out life's next move. He was a veteran of several other hikes throughout the Cascades and Olympics, so we shared some of our favorite places we had hiked the past years. Seven Lakes Basin in the Olympics, Spider Meadow, and Spider Gap in the Cascades were among the most memorable.

Sam was somewhat of an anomaly on the PCT with respect to the age. So far it seemed that most PCT hikers were somewhere between twenty-one and thirty years of age. I think the reasons for that age group are obvious. A few hikers were in their thirties, but then the age groups bounced up to hikers in their late fifties. At the time I met Sam, I had not met anyone in his sixties or seventies. Hiking the PCT takes time. Most people in their forties and fifties are not able to take that much time off from their careers or families. For that group, hiking the PCT is simply a distant fantasy that would have to be put on hold for many years. Most individuals in the sixty-to-seventy age group find they are unable to maintain the physical rigor and difficulty of the PCT. I counted myself exceedingly fortunate to be in good enough shape to do the hike. So meeting Sam was an atypical encounter. He was between careers, his children were raised and on their own, and his wife, an employee of REI, was totally supportive of his adventure.

At around eleven o'clock, I was getting antsy to get on the trail. I wanted to reach the Pass sooner rather than later. I put away my trail mix, filled my water bottle with lake water, and announced I would be on my way. I asked if he wanted to hike together for a few miles. He declined, explaining that his son was going to meet him at the trailhead at Snoqualmie Pass and he wanted to time this day of hiking so he would come off the trail right where his son was parked within a few minutes of his arrival. I figured, given his age and his obvious good health, he would catch up with me soon enough, so we said our goodbyes and I headed down the trail that clung closely to the lake for about a half a mile before heading northeast.

Just as I expected, Sam caught up about seven miles from the Pass. We hiked for about an hour together, but he soon needed to pick up his pace in order to meet his son at the time they had arranged. Besides, the big toe on my left foot was in so much pain; there was no way I was going to maintain his pace. Even so, it was good to have someone to chat with along the trail, and I figured I would see him before the end of my hike. He planned to get off the trail at Snoqualmie Pass, head home for some personal business, and then start again from the Pass in about a week. Given the pace he kept, I figured we would likely meet up again sometime between Stevens Pass and Stehekin, where he planned to join his wife and stay at one of the lodges.

Around 5:00 p.m., I walked down the mountain towards Snoqualmie Pass, the same side of the mountain where the winter snow draws hordes of skiers throughout the winter months. I walked under the cables of the ski lifts towards the parking lot and saw Sam sitting with his son who, indeed, had brought a cooler of his favorite beer, fresh fruit, and assorted cheeses and chips. As I came closer, I saw them waving me towards them. I stepped up my pace and eagerly approached. Sam had a very satisfied look on his face. Most likely he was into his second beer. His son reached out his hand towards me holding a bottle of beer dripping with ice from the cooler. It was tempting. In a split second I thought, who would ever know or care? But I settled for one of the cold sodas still embedded in the ice. Off went The Rock and I plunked down in utter exhaustion but with a sense of satisfaction that I had just completed the 100 miles between White Pass and Snoqualmie Pass and the 250 miles from the Columbia Gorge. Not counting the zero days taken, I had hiked for twenty days.

I sat on the pavement of the parking lot with Sam and his son for about a half hour before excusing myself, then walked alongside Highway 90 towards the motel a hundred yards up the road. In the short time I had been sitting with Sam and his son, my body had seized up, and the pain in my foot was causing me to limp. With The Rock on my back and my crooked gait, I must have looked like a cripple just out of his casts or an old man best served sitting in a wheelchair. I felt even worse.

I checked into one of the rooms the motel held especially for PCT hikers and retrieved the reload box that was waiting for me behind the counter. Once again, Carla had added a few extra goodies and a sweet note of encouragement: *Hope this finds you in good health and spirits. I'm amazed at your determination and proud of your tenacity. Be safe. I keep forgetting to water the container plants. I may have killed a few. Sorry! I miss you.* Her note brought a smile to my weary face. She also packed my cell phone so I could call her when I had a clearer sense when I'd reach my next stop, Stevens Pass. The plan was for her to meet me at Skykomish with my next reload box.

I quickly settled into my room, plugged my phone into the charger, took off my boots, put on my sandals, and headed back outside where I had seen several PCT hikers gathering on the side of the small convenient store. By then, Sam and his son had joined them and were offering everyone something from the cooler. Sam was another in a long line of generous people I had met along the trail.

Within the hour, Hank and Robbie came riding off the trail leading the two mules tethered close behind. They rode towards the parking lot adjacent to the store. Almost simultaneously, a large pickup truck with a massive horse trailer came roaring up the road and parked about a hundred feet from where our group was gathered. I figured it had to be Hank's wife come to collect Hank and Robbie and the four animals. I broke away from the group and walked towards the two men. Robbie saw me coming, jumped off his horse, and walked swiftly towards me. About five feet away, he broke out into a huge grin, grabbed me in a huge bear hug, and lifted me off the ground. We both laughed and, arm in arm, headed back towards the trailer where his grandparents were standing.

As we walked, Robbie explained that he and Hank had found a meadow about a half mile off the trail with a small lake nearby. That's where they had camped and why I had missed them. The noise from the bells had been muffled by a bank of trees and my own noisy rattling of pack and gear. Hank said he was worried that something had happened, because the last time he'd seen me I was helping Rich make his way up the trail. Robbie said he was worried he wouldn't see me again. It was a very sweet moment for the three of us, but it was short-lived.

Hank's wife was anxious to load the stock and head back home—about a three-hour drive. Once again we said our goodbyes, gave one another hugs, and exchanged phone numbers and addresses. I walked back toward the group of hikers as my friends drove east towards home. I felt a little sad about their departure. They had shown me incredible generosity and kindness as we had shared campfires, life stories, cigars, food, and a whole lot of laughter—as long as we stayed clear of politics!

I headed back to my motel room to rest and write in my journal before I forgot some details of the day.

Journal Entry:
Sam and his son left about an hour ago, and according to his schedule, I may meet up with him again. Perhaps at Stevens Pass, but for certain at Stehekin.

Called the family today and brought them up to date on my whereabouts. No one seemed particularly concerned that anything bad might have happened. A good thing because I don't want them to worry about me. Each expressed profuse congratulations and relief!

For some reason, people think I'm going to fall off some cliff or be swallowed whole by an army of marauding bears. I don't get that close to cliffs and there are no man-eating bears in these parts. If seen at all, the black bears in the Cascades are primarily berry gatherers. If they are not disturbed or don't sense their cubs are in danger, no harm comes to a hiker. They are large and magnificent. Why would I ever want to shoot one?

Had dinner tonight at the restaurant attached to the motel with "Platypus," a thirty-something dentist from San Diego. She's a thru hiker doing about forty miles a day. She's been giving away most of her foodstuffs so she can get her pack down to about twenty pounds. Crazy lady!

Just took a very long shower, shaved, and put all my clothes in the dryer. When dry, will drop into bed and sleep long into the morning. May not take two full zero days.

Some random thoughts before the day is done:

"I am exceedingly grateful for this experience."

"I take none of it for granted."

"I could not be out here without Carla's support."

"I am grateful for all my childhood mentors who taught me to love the wilderness, to explore places that few people have ever been, to respect the mountains, to love God for giving it to us to steward wisely."

***

That night was the first time in over three weeks I had slept in a real bed. It felt wonderful. A younger and tougher man would have been up at the first sign of light, packed up, scarfed down an ample breakfast at the adjacent café, and been on the trail by seven. Not me. I am no longer young and I make no claims at toughness. So I lay in bed and considered the option of staying one more day and leaving the next morning. It took me about ten seconds to decide. I rolled over on my other side, fluffed up the two pillows, and went back to sleep.

In my defense, I needed to contact REI about my damaged backpack that was the cause of some extremely uncomfortable hours of hiking. Apparently the fastener on one of the straps was broken, so I couldn't get The Rock tight enough to keep it from dragging on my lower back. I needed to wait until REI opened so I could ask about a replacement pack. Unless I was willing to get off the trail, travel down Highway 90 into the Seattle area for an exchange, then back to Snoqualmie Pass—a time-frame of about two days—I would have to keep the pack I already had and exchange it when I reached Stevens Pass about a hundred miles north. After several minutes of discussing the problem and the options with someone at the Alderwood REI store, we agreed that a new, equivalent pack would be sent to my home and someone from home could bring it to me when I reached Stevens Pass. The folks at REI were understanding and accommodating beyond all my expectations.

I spent Day Twenty-Four just hanging out around the motel, reading old newspapers left behind, writing in my journal, and eating as much junk food as my system could tolerate. At this juncture I figured I had lost about ten pounds, so wasn't concerned about all the extra calories I was consuming.

Over the course of the day, I repacked my backpack at least twice so that any item I decided was unnecessary was sent back home—extra batteries, more than two pairs of socks, food beyond six trail days, an extra headlamp, a book I had yet to read, deodorant—and I stayed off my feet as much as possible. An extra day of pampering would have a noticeable payoff.

***

Snoqualmie Pass is a place I have driven through on my way eastward over the past thirty-plus years. But this was the first time I had stayed overnight or longer than a couple hours. Whenever my family or I drove east of the Cascades on Highway 90, we would usually stop for breakfast at the same restaurant where I was now eating. It felt strange that I was here without them.

The last time I remember being here was with Carla and Noah when we drove him to Whitman College in Walla Walla to begin his freshman year. We stopped for breakfast and a pit stop. I remember sitting across from my

144 ~ G. William Jolley

son and feeling a hint of sadness. I remembered having a clear sense that this would be among the few times we would do this routine again. He would graduate, go on to graduate school, settle into a career, find new friends and new residences, and move further from his mother and me on his own pathway to independence and adulthood. It would all happen too soon. I felt a little cheated. He wasn't supposed to grow up so quickly. It seemed that last week he was a squeaky little boy running around the property announcing in the midst of his busyness that he was a "worker guy." A lot of years have passed since then in such a short time.

I finished my breakfast and was lingering over another cup of coffee while writing in my journal. I had no plans except to rest and prepare for the following day when I would get back on the trail. The waitress poured more coffee into my cup, and I stared out the window. I thought of the times when all four of my children and I backpacked and camped in the Cascades and Olympics. I started them young, and we continued to share those experiences until just recently when they all found other ways to spend their summers or found other friends to share the backpacking. It was an inevitable transition, but I missed it. I missed being in the mountains with them and all the goofy, quirky, and memorable moments we shared.

One such time was when Jonah thought he would do me a favor and dry my wet hiking pants. It had rained earlier that particular day and he, his bother Noah, and I sat huddled on a boulder on the top of Spider Ridge under a tarp too small to completely cover all three of us to wait out the rain. But he placed my pants too close to the flames and they ignited. I was away from the campsite fetching water from the nearby stream, and when I returned, Jonah was in tears. I think he was afraid I was going to feed him to the bears. But I told him he did me a great favor because I never did like those pants anyway. Burning them actually gave me a green light to purchase another pair when I returned home. The incident was a gentle moment of relief and forgiveness.

I chuckled to myself, thinking I'd missed the memo about my children actually growing up and moving out, and that our lives would be lived so separately. That's a good thing, but still, sitting at that table, staring into the coffee cup and considering all of it, I didn't like it. I wanted my kids back.

***

I saw Platypus standing outside the convenience store about a hundred feet away. I was still sitting in the restaurant and looking out the window. I wasn't going to drink any more coffee, but I wasn't ready to leave either. I waved to her as she hoisted her pack onto her back and headed towards the trailhead about half a mile north from where she was standing.

Her room had been next to mine, so we had spoken a few times in the hallway. The previous evening, she had left her door open, and I could see into her room. She had a pile of food on her bed that she was sorting out. About half of it she wasn't taking but wasn't sure what to leave behind in the hiker's box. She offered some of it to me, but I was also trying to find ways to lessen my load. Even with all my own winnowing and sorting, I was still going to carry a forty-pound pack. The rub was that she covered around forty miles a day and would be at Stevens Pass in less than three days. That same 100 miles would take me at least seven to eight days, requiring more food and, consequently, more weight. I stood by the bed and watched her make choices about what to keep and what to give away. It was an interesting exercise in how we each made choices about what we thought we needed to bring on the PCT, knowing that whatever decision we made had to stick because there was no turning back. Once on the trail, we had to live with our choices, with the stuff we packed, and with the weight.

When I waved to her from the window that morning, I knew I would not see her again. She was another among the many PCT hikers I had met, enjoyed a brief moment in time, swapped a few stories, shared a meal or two with, expressed words of safety and blessings to, and waved farewell. I was still thinking about Hank and Robbie and their horses and mules. I would miss them.

23

FROM PASS—

On the morning of Day Twenty-Five, I hung around Snoqualmie Pass waiting for the post office to open so I could send home all the items I'd decided unnecessary and would add more weight to my pack. Though I sent back close to ten pounds, The Rock still weighed about forty pounds. I couldn't seem to get the damned thing any lighter, especially at the beginning of a section with all the food and equipment for the next stage. A long section required a lot of supplies.

The postal worker was on his own agenda and didn't open for business until nearly 10:00 a.m. I finally got the package in the mail, bought a cup of coffee at the gas station along with some nondescript bakery item, and headed towards the trailhead a quarter mile down Highway 90. This was the first day since leaving the Columbia Gorge that I hiked in cloudy and threatening weather.

According to the map, this would be among the most difficult days of hiking along the Washington section. Snoqualmie Pass is at 3,000 feet elevation, and where I planned to finish the day, eight miles north, was at 5,500 feet, a 2,500 foot rise in elevation. Rudimentary math informed me I would be hiking on steep switchbacks for the remainder of the day. But again, it was simply one step at a time. When the trail got too difficult, I walked slower, took more breaks, and recalibrated the miles I chose to hike. In this section, slower could actually be better because I had entered the Alpine Lakes Wilderness, one of the most beautiful areas in the entire country. This was a section I didn't want to blast through. As if I even could!

At around 5:30 p.m., I decided to call it quits for the day. I had hiked just shy of eight miles, but the next place to camp where there was water was eight miles north and there was no way I could make that distance before nightfall.

There was plenty of space by Ridge Lake, and less than fifty yards from where I camped was Gravel Lake. I had my pick of lakes that evening. A rare choice to have. Within a few minutes, a woman in her early- to mid-fifties came off the trail and headed towards where I sat. She looked more beat-up than me, so I offered her a cup of tea, which she accepted. Like me, she planned to camp by Ridge Lake rather than attempt to make it to Park Lake, several miles away. She was impressed when I told her that I often ended a long day of hiking with a cup of tea with sugar. I told her it seemed a civilized thing to do.

Sue started hiking the PCT in her mid-twenties but, in her words, "life got in the way," and she abandoned further hikes until her last child left home, which soon was followed by the sudden death of her husband. It was then she decided to take a section each year until she had completed the entire PCT. The section between Snoqualmie Pass and Stevens Pass was the last section left on her list. Sipping her tea, she declared with the enthusiasm of a teenager that once she reached Stevens Pass, she would have hiked the entire trail. We raised our cups in a toast to her success.

About fifty feet beyond where we sat, there was a large, flat, open area adjacent to a small clump of scrubby pine trees. Sue thanked me for the tea, set her cup by my feet, and walked over towards the area that appeared to be a promising spot for her to pitch a tent. About two minutes later I heard her yell, "Fuck!"

"What's going on?" I yelled as I jumped up. In so doing, I knocked over her cup.

"Someone's taken some big dumps right here in the middle of this great camping spot and left it," she yelled back at me.

I walked towards her but stopped short. I had no need to gaze upon someone's pile of crap. Sue came roaring back towards me in a posture of fury.

"Who the hell leaves their shit for everyone else to deal with?" She wasn't speaking metaphorically.

"Beats me." I paused and looked her way. "Miscreants. Amateurs who have no respect for the mountains."

"I can't camp down there, and I'm sure as hell not going to deal with those piles."

"Well, it's getting late in the season, so there probably won't be that many hikers between now and the winter snows. Hopefully the piles will be gone by next year."

"Well, that's no comfort for me."

Sue was not going to let this go easily, and I saw no need to make excuses for someone else's disgusting behavior. I boiled more water for tea, and after we had sat for a few minutes waiting for the tea to cool, I said, "That wasn't the doing of a PCTer. Had to be a day hiker or someone camping for the night from Snoqualmie Pass. I refuse to accept that anyone hiking the PCT would be responsible for that."

I wanted to believe that *no* human would be so thoughtless, because everyone owed God the decency to behave with extraordinary care in the wilderness, which is why most backpackers carry a small plastic trowel to dig a hole so they can bury their poop. Simply placing a few twigs or a rock over the waste doesn't cut it in the wilderness.

We finished our tea and exhausted the subject of backpack etiquette and then agreed Sue would pitch her tent about twenty feet from mine. Later that evening, we sat together and shared dinner along with stories of our lives and marriages, children, and careers. It was another among many random and pleasant encounters I enjoyed with total strangers.

***

Early the next morning on Day Twenty-Six, Sue was up. I stayed in my tent and heard her rustling around with preparations for breakfast and eventual packing. The morning was cloudy and misty, and I wasn't in any hurry to leave the warmth, so I unzipped my tent, poked my head out, and wished her well on the last miles of her hike. Within a few minutes she was on her way and I didn't meet up with her again.

I had slept well that night, even though the wind blew pretty fiercely. I boiled water for hot cocoa then got back into my tent out of the cold morning air, lay on one side, and leafed through a few pages of my journal.

Journal Entry:
Yesterday on the trail I could look down towards the east and see Lake Kachess, an area where Noah and I took a day hike last summer. We had planned to hike the Seven Lakes Basin loop. I had done it with Jonah when he was just twelve, but Noah had never been in that area of the Olympics. I got a DUI and was in an outpatient treatment program that required I be present during the time we had planned our hike. For part of today, those feelings of remorse and being a royal fuck-up felt like a knife in my gut. I try not to go into those places too often. Don't see the point of it. Just beats me up. But it is an appropriate reminder that my drinking has caused a lot of grief to my family and there is no way I can make any of that go away. I wonder if Noah and I will ever make that hike to Seven Lakes Basin. I wonder if Noah will ever be okay with the disappointments I have created in his life. I wonder what will become of my relationship with Noah. I wonder.

I've got to get out of this tent and get on the trail or I'll never make it to Stevens Pass.

Seventy miles to go.

That day I hoped to hike fourteen miles, but the reality was that the trail was a series of formidable switchbacks along with large boulders that took a lot out of me to climb over and around. The switchbacks were murder on my COPD, and by the end of any day, the boulders were killers for my knees. The younger hikers would merely skip from one boulder to the next like mountain goats. This old goat had to gingerly maneuver them with careful calculations so I wouldn't slip and fall. Falling from a boulder with The Rock on my back could spell disaster for me. So it was slow going and lower mileage.

The foggy morning lent an eerie quiet along the trail. I hiked alone for several miles then came to Jo and Edds Lakes, several hundred yards apart and down into steep gullies. I didn't want to take the extra effort to hike down to them. I was ready for a break, so I sat on the stump of an old cedar tree and stared at their deep blue waters. I was also ready for some water and a protein bar, and it was a good time to jot something in my journal. I sat rereading some of my entries from the morning as I had lay in my tent keeping warm and sipping hot cocoa. I rarely think about my stepfather anymore, but reading my journal entries about Noah brought him to mind. Comparisons are not usually a healthy exercise, but I couldn't keep my mind from drifting down that pathway. Besides, I had twelve miles and the entire rest of the day to ponder, so what better subject than father-son relationships?

***

It was 1960 in mid-January. I remember the ringing of the phone that jarred me out of my Saturday morning slumber and my slipper-less feet plodding along the cold tiled floor towards the kitchen. My mother was slumped over the stove. I can still conjure up her look of total dismay and shock as she quietly uttered, "Daddy's gone."

My first impulse was to ask, "Gone where?" Even at seventeen, I possessed an advanced level of sarcasm that protected me from a harsh truth I wanted to hold at bay. But in that moment, the truth I could not hold back was that my dad was not coming home from the hospital, where he had been recovering from a minor heart attack. I knew that, within a few days, the hospital bed Mother had ordered, the one that was sitting in their bedroom, would be returned, and I knew that my father and I would never speak again. What I had taken for granted most my life was forever snatched from me in a twinkling of an eye.

Mother turned around and moved a few feet, where she stood almost catatonic leaning against the refrigerator. I stumbled my way to the breakfast nook, sat dazed, and quietly, and with a hoarse morning voice, I asked in a near whisper, "What now?"

I don't remember my mother responding. Probably because she hadn't a clue. It felt as if the room were filled with a thick substance that kept the two of us immobilized. As if time had stopped. Maybe it was the heaviness of inexplicable fear and grief. I wanted to return to bed, curl up, and wait for better news or until I awoke from this nightmare. As I was about to lift myself from where I sat, my eight-year-old sister stood at the doorway asking what was wrong. The next thing I remember was her falling on the kitchen floor in a heap of sobs, gasping for breath.

Dad wasn't supposed to die. He was fifty-two years of age and had made promises to put aside his two-pack-a-day habit and lose weight. He was supposed to reduce his intake of all the crappy, fatty food he consumed by the ton and lower his blood pressure. Dad was still relatively young, my mother was forty, my brother was twenty, my sister was eight, and I was seventeen. He left us grieving that morning and for hundreds of mornings to come. That morning I hated him more for being selfish than for leaving me steeped in sorrow.

That was what I recalled while I sat on the cedar log by the side of the trail, chewing on a protein bar and staring down at the calm surface of Jo Lake. It still remains a mystery how we all survived those first several weeks after Dad's death. I'm sure all the details between his body lying in a hospital bed and the funeral home where he lay before the memorial service were daunting. But I was not privy to any of that. I was far too enmeshed in my own grief to see beyond my bedroom, where I holed up for the next month.

His body was dressed and prepared for "viewing" at the Pierce Brothers Funeral Home somewhere in Hollywood. Against my brother's and my protestations, my mother settled on the cheapest casket offered, and there my father lay for two days prior to the funeral. On the night before the service, I drove the thirty miles from our house to the funeral home. I vividly remember walking quietly towards the casket. I stood over Dad's body that was dressed in his favorite gray suit, a starched white dress shirt with a tie my mother had carefully chosen from his closet. I gently placed my right open hand on his chest and spoke quietly to him.

"Dad, it's time to come home."

No response.

"Wake up, Dad, we need you home. Mom is already going crazy, Missy can't stop sobbing, Gaylord's gone AWOL, and I can't imagine our home without you."

No response.

I stood over his silent, impeccably dressed form, his lifeless, breathless body, and slowly lifted my hand from his chest. I waited, hoping that magically his eyes would open and he'd instruct me to get him out of that goddamned cheap box and get the fuck out of there. But that didn't happen, and I left him lying there, alone. I returned to my car and drove home through the darkness and rain.

No matter how I processed and configured all of the information around his death, I couldn't reconcile how I could have visited him one night then be told the very next morning he was dead. None of it made any sense. And the harder I attempted to make some sense of it, the more I plunged into sadness and confusion. Thinking back on that horrible time in my young life, I realize that my feelings may not have even been about Dad's passing. It may have been more about remorse that at that time we had been so alienated and distant. At that age, I didn't even have a sensible way of thinking about it. Hell, I didn't even have the vocabulary to talk about it. It was just an onerous and painful thing that happened in my young life. It is no hyperbole that every day for the next two months I wept inconsolably.

Though my mother eventually remarried and led a relatively happy and contented life, I believe she always kept my dad tucked safely in a part of her heart and from time to time would return to that place and remember. He was her one true love.

Maybe thinking about the loss of my father was why I anxiously fretted about Noah's and my relationship. I felt a palpable fear at the possibility that I would die before we had made our peace with one another. There was even a tinge of drama to it: I needed to get off the trail, rush to him, embrace him, shake him, and tell him we must make things right, that we were running out of time, and that I would not allow him to live with those same feelings of remorse and "unfinished business" I have carried most my life.

I was a high school senior when my father died, full of my own importance and living a life that distanced my parents as far as possible. A father/adolescent-son disconnect is as common as winter snow in the Cascades, but the frozen spaces between my father and me never thawed. We never arrived at that place where I experienced him as a normal human being alongside all the other men in their fifties working hard to support families and doing the best they could to love their wives and parent their children. I was stuck in a constant state of resentment about everything from his being "uncool" to his last haircut to his goofy-looking glasses to his being a dad who never took me camping or fishing to his lame jokes. He simply wasn't the father I would have picked.

But in truth, he picked me.

Shortly after he married my mother, he adopted my brother and me. William Albert Jolley from Roodhouse, Illinois became an instant father of two sons and the only father I ever knew. When I was born, my birth father was "at sea" and didn't return until I was nearly three. I have no memory of him. What remained a mystery is that my mother had my birth certificate altered to indicate that Jolley was my birth father. My brother and I never thought of him as a "step" father. He was simply "Dad."

I didn't want to forget some of what I had been remembering about those days and feelings around the time of my father's death, so I grabbed another protein bar from my food sack, took out my journal, and spent the next half hour writing entries.

Journal Entry:
I wonder what my life would have been had Dad lived. Would I have gone on to conservatory and studied piano? Would I have married so young? Would we have reconciled our relationship and become friends? If he were alive, would he be proud of me?

I don't think my mother ever recovered from her grief. I think she longed for his friendship and partnership until the day she died, even though she did remarry. I wish she were still alive so I could ask her. I know she'd tell me.

There are times when I wonder if I have spent most my life in search of the approval I wanted from a father who died too soon. There were so many times in years past I needed him to give me direction and counsel. Sometimes I feel I've been adrift and making choices I had no business making on my own.

***

I was thoughtful and sad the rest of the day. Those memories took a lot of energy out of me, and I felt tired as the day and mileage dragged on. Nevertheless, I hiked a good distance and around 6:00 p.m. started looking for a place to stop for the night. I wanted to camp at Delete Creek, but the one camping space along the creek just a few feet from the bridge that crossed it was already taken by a man whose large black dog was lying on a blanket next to his tent. The man looked up when he heard me coming down the trail.

He told me his dog had rubbed his paws raw on all the rocks and couldn't walk any farther. The dog weighed around eighty pounds and there was no way he could carry the animal down the trail, so he had been camping there for the past couple days hoping the dog would recover enough to begin walking again. He asked if I had any books I could leave with him because he was bored silly from just sitting all day. I told him I didn't pack any books except my small, portable copy of the New Testament. He said he didn't want a Bible because he wasn't religious.

I just shrugged my shoulders and hiked on for another mile until I found a small place alongside the trail where I could pitch my tent. The trail followed close to Delete Creek, and the rushing water was so noisy, that I could hear the roar from my campsite.

I felt badly for the man with the dog, but I didn't offer to help lug his eighty-pound pet down the trail. Maybe that's what he actually wanted but didn't ask. According to my map, unless he backtracked about twenty miles to Snoqualmie Pass or went ahead another sixty miles to Stevens Pass, he didn't have any other options but to wait until his dog recovered. That incident was another reason I knew I would never backpack with a dog.

I made a quick dinner, changed into my sleeping clothes, and crawled into the tent for the night. It was nearly dark, so I put on my headlight and wrote in my journal.

Journal Entry:
Today I miss Carla more than any other day since I left.
I hiked around twelve miles today, but it felt like fifteen. Probably because most of it was up on switchbacks. Just a major grind. Need a good night's sleep so I can start tomorrow rested with a clearer head.

I could hear the loud sound of rushing water as I zipped the flap on my tent and clicked off my headlamp. Except for the man and his lame dog, I had not seen anyone the entire day. It was a good day to be silent, to reflect, and to hike alone.

***

Day Twenty-Seven began with clear, sunny skies and the promise of a dry, hot day. The day before had been a bitch of a hike, with so many switchbacks that I lost count. The last two miles down to Delete Creek were a body-jarring 2,000-foot drop over rocks and exposed tree roots that I kept tripping on. I lost track of how many times I stubbed the toes of my boots. And every time I did, an intensely sharp pain shot through my feet up to my knees. Fortunately, I packed ample Aleve and was devouring them like M&Ms.

Well, it was a new day and I figured it couldn't get any more difficult than the day before, so I began with a high level of optimism. Short-lived it turned out. In about three miles I came to Lemah Creek, a broad, deep, roaring river where the remnants of a bridge stood as testimony that even the most solid of structures are no match for floods that come crashing down the valley, taking everything in their wake. The bridge had been washed out for several years, and only a fallen tree about fifty feet downriver served as a means of crossing from one shore to the other. It was a pretty substantial log that lay about four feet above the water. To slip and fall off the log could mean a violent and swift trip downstream.

From where I stood on the bank, I could see to the other side, where a couple had made camp and were watching me as I removed my pack and considered my limited options about how to cross this roaring, swift body of water. The man yelled over to me, "The log is pretty sturdy and the creek is too deep to walk across. No rocks to use as stepping stones."

I yelled back over the roar, "I was hoping for an easier day!"

"Start across the log and I'll come down your way in case you get into trouble."

I hated crossing creeks, streams, or rivers over logs. Even with my ever-trusty trekking poles, a crossing was always a challenge and a time for constant mantras to convince myself I was up to the challenge. I needed all the help I could get from the poles and God and the spirits of the mountains. Mostly, it was a matter of simply girding my cowardly loins and forging ahead. Sometimes there was a crude but obvious pathway of rocks stretching from one side to the other. But most times I had to make my peace with a fallen tree as the only option. Either way, with one eye, my balance was sketchy and unpredictable. It was never a certainty I could get across without slipping. There were times when walking across a particular log was too scary, so I'd scoot across on my butt, with my feet dangling in the frigid water. "Better to have wet boots than fall in and have everything in my pack dripping wet," I would tell myself. I also told myself that no one was likely to come along and lift me and The Rock to the other side. So I could stand by the water and procrastinate and work myself into a froth of worry and anxiety, or I could get on with it.

Setting aside my fears, I hoisted The Rock on my back, strapped it particularly tight, took several very deep breaths, said a couple quiet prayers, and headed for the log about fifty feet down from where I stood. It was an enormous tree that looked as though it had been uprooted by a flood. The roots were shooting every which way while the top of the tree was lying on the other side of the creek. I had to use the roots as handles to hoist myself up on the log to begin my initial, cautious steps. I looked down the log towards the other side about thirty feet away. Thirty feet of walking on a ten-inch-round surface, one boot over the other, my trekking poles dangling over the sides with nowhere to place them on anything solid. With my pack and its broken strap, a roaring, boiling stream below, and about fifteen feet left before I could feel the safety of solid ground, I slipped! As I felt my boots leave the log and my body about to crash into the water, by some mysterious, last second effort, I twisted myself around so that I fell facing the log and grabbed it as if my life depended on holding on. My lower body and legs felt the ice-cold water rush by.

Within seconds, and with a Herculean effort, I hoisted myself back on top of the log and there I sat, trembling from shock and cold. My heart was beating so fast I was certain it would come crashing out of my chest and float down the stream. I took several deep breaths to calm myself before deciding on my next move. At least I was facing in the right direction. By then, the man who had yelled at me about using the log for crossing the stream ran down to the end of the fallen tree. He climbed onto the log and with a sturdy, youthful, and fearless act of bravery, stood over me and hoisted me back on my feet, never letting go of my arms so that I could use his strength for the remainder of the crossing. He was a bona fide Trail Angel!

I followed Joe back to his campsite, where his wife had witnessed the entire incident and was waiting with a hot cup of coffee for me. Two Trail Angels in one meeting. Wet and cold and still a bit shaken, I still felt that a great fortune had befallen me. I took off my boots and socks, placed them close to the fire still glowing and warm at midmorning, and sat basking in the warmth of safety, hospitality, and coffee.

Their camp sat where the bridge used to begin. It was a flat, spacious area surrounded by beautiful fir trees and protective shrubs that invited a camper to stay longer than just a quick stopover. I wanted just that, to stay longer, but felt compelled to get several more miles behind me before the end of the day. I was already a full day behind from where I had told Carla I would be to arrive at Stevens Pass in time for her to meet me with my new pack. I didn't want to fall further behind and worry her. There was no phone reception in this area, so there was no way I could contact her. I simply had to get back on the trail and make up as much time as possible. Joe and his wife and their cozy campsite were lovely and inviting, but I had a great distance yet to go. And I had a 2,300 elevation switchback to climb to get to Escondido Ridge. It was only eight miles away, but it was a rugged, demanding eight miles.

They offered me another cup of coffee and some of her homemade trail mix. I sat awhile longer, allowing more time for my boots to dry. Joe and I concurred that to fix the bridge would take about ten college kids, one engineering student, and two weeks to design and build so that log across the roaring, boiling stream could be avoided. But even after over eight years of a destroyed bridge, the government couldn't figure out how to organize such an endeavor. Hell, Joe and I agreed we'd volunteer our time to organize the entire project. We had a good laugh about how things that appear so direct and simple seem to become so complicated and convoluted. We noted that is why hiking the PCT is so appealing: Everything is simple and direct and uncomplicated. You arise in the morning and walk and everything else really doesn't much matter. I wanted to stay longer, but my boots were dry enough to pull over my semi-dry socks, and my body had recovered from its trauma. We said our goodbyes and I was off, headed towards Escondido Ridge. The rest of the day went without incident. Aside from Joe and his wife, I met no one else that day.

Though only ten miles of hiking, as I expected, it was a hard day of uphill and switchbacks. By 4:00 p.m. I decided I had hiked as far as my body would take me. I would have liked a better spot to camp, but I would have had to cover another five to eight miles and I didn't want to hike much longer. So, it was a short day. I found a secluded area next to a partially snow-covered tarn where the mountain came directly down to its shore. It was a beautiful site, though very buggy and a bit soggy from a snowmelt that seemed late for this time of year. Because I was at the foot of a mountain and I was camped at around 6,000 feet, I knew that once the sun started setting, it was going to be cold. I scoured the area for about an hour and collected an ample pile of dry wood for the evening and morning campfire.

Journal Entry:
Feels like it will be a cold night tonight. The gentle breeze is coming off the snowfields just a few yards from where I'm camped.

Super buggy as it gets closer to nightfall. Have lit a tattered cigar that seems to discourage them from getting too close. Given the stench of my stogy and my own body, I wouldn't get close to me either.

I'm glad that I decided to call it a good day of hiking. This is a perfect place to camp, though the ground's a bit mushy. Good I brought the ground cover. Not that much more weight for all the benefits.

I wish Carla was sitting next to me right now, though she wouldn't be putting up with any cigar smoking!

So I ask myself a physics questions: When, if I keep hiking up, up, up, will I ever start hiking down, down, down? Where's Noah when I need him? He and Jonah would love this experience, though they would never have stopped here. They would have hiked another five to eight miles. Another reason to hike alone.

***

On Day Twenty-Eight, I hiked eleven hours and arrived at Deep Lake at the foot of Cathedral Pass four miles to the north. I could see the pass from where I camped. It stood majestic with its sharp peaks showing off the brilliant white of snow that refused to melt even late into summer. There was a prohibition from camping too close to the lake, so I set up camp about a hundred yards away. That was fine by me because the closer I got to the lake, the buggier it got. The camping areas were large and flat and appeared overused. Some of them looked as if they had accommodated horse campers who packed into this area for hunting season. Right about then I wouldn't have minded a horse to ride.

The wood sources were pretty picked-over, but I scoured the area around my site and was able to collect a large enough pile for a substantial fire. Anyone reading this, you might say, "Holy crap, this guy does the same thing every frick'n day: hikes, breaks for water, eats, collects wood, pitches a tent, lights a fire, drinks tea, eats dinner, writes in a journal, goes to bed, and wakes up the next morning to do it all over again." And that person would be correct. Every day was pretty much the same. To which I would say, "And aren't I the fortunate one? Because there is something very comforting about the sort of routine I experience on the trail. Very few surprises, and no drama of my own making, beauty at nearly every turn in the trail, one dish to wash, no laundry, no lawn to mow, no TV, no political debates to suffer through, no cell phones or computers. Just a study in routine and consistency and simplicity. A person should try it at least once in a lifetime."

What didn't feel like beauty and simplicity today was the fact that I fell twice! And I fell hard. I tripped over a small, unobtrusive rock protruding out of the trail, twice within an hour, both times while looking out at the scenery. Though I had tripped too many times to count on any given day, I had yet to actually tumble. And, with The Rock on my back driving my body into the ground, it truly hurt.

The second time I fell was just after lunch. I was looking at a distant peak when I caught my foot on a protruding root and this time fell off the trail about fifteen feet down a slope. Fortunately, my fall was stopped by a small stump jutting out of the side of the hill. It all happened so quickly and without anticipation that when I stopped with my body jammed against the stump, I had to think for a second where I was. Was any part of me broken or damaged and, mostly, how the hell was I going to get back on my feet and back on the trail?

I lay on my side where I had stopped and considered my options. I was in such an awkward position I realized there was no possibility of removing my pack. Hell, even if I wanted to, I couldn't reach the straps. I realized, with the pack holding me down as if someone were sitting on top of me, I didn't have much leverage to rise up. And if I did rise up without caution, I might dislodge the stump and could tumble even farther down the hill. At that moment I felt genuinely screwed. Of course, I thought about the possibility of remaining stationary and waiting until another hiker came along to rescue me. But a wait could take the remainder of the day. That didn't seem a viable option.

By then I had been lying against the stump for about five minutes when I just decided to let all hell break loose, take a couple of deep breaths, and make one huge effort to pull myself away from the stump towards the trail and get my feet back under me. And that is exactly what I did and did it with definitive aplomb. I was back on the trail! A little beat up and worn down, yet safe, with nothing broken or bruised except my pride. And I admit, once back on the trail, I did look around to see if anyone had witnessed my clumsy moment.

But I was exhausted both from sheer terror and fright, as well as the physical toll it had taken to get off the side of the cliff. With The Rock next to me, I sat on the side of the trail looking down at the tree stump that had kept me from tumbling down another three hundred feet to the rocky bottom of the ravine. It was then that my body was consumed by a wave of nausea as I considered what might or even should have happened.

In two days I had fallen three times. Once into a roaring creek and twice along the trail. What was next? I was afraid to hazard a guess.

***

I had finished my dinner, so planned to get into the tent and end the day earlier than usual, if for no other reason than to escape the pesky bugs that no doubt had signaled to their cohorts that I had finished my cigar and the coast was clear. Above their buzzing, I heard some rattling coming from down the trail. With the campfire reduced to embers, I couldn't see a thing. Then suddenly I heard a woman's voice call out, "Can I come into your camp?"

"Come ahead," I shouted back over my shoulder. Though I could hear her clanging towards me, I still couldn't see her. "I'll throw on more wood," I called out again. Within a few seconds I could see her headlamp bobbing towards me. Another few seconds, she emerged from the darkness.

"Oh my God, I'm glad to find someone. I thought I was lost but couldn't find any place to camp." She was standing over me as she spoke. I invited her to drop her pack and sit by the fire. She immediately plopped down in exhaustion. "I think I hiked about thirty miles today."

"Only thirty?" I laughed.

"Some days I've hiked as much as forty," she quickly responded, a little defensively.

"You're welcome to stay here for the night. Plenty of room."

"Thanks, I think I will. I don't like hiking in the dark."

"No one should be out in these mountains in the dark. It's a very bad idea." My paternal self kicked in.

She told me her trail name but within minutes I forgot it and didn't want to ask again. She was from North Carolina and worked in a non-profit Christian organization. I wanted to comment about the redundancy of her words but considered she might not see the humor in my linguistic purity so I let it slide.

As a thru hiker, she had devised a rather clever strategy of receiving her reload packages. Apparently, where she attended church, she asked various groups to send her packages on the basis of the information she left with them about the kinds of food she needed, the amount of gas for her stove she required, and other assorted gear such as socks, shoelaces, clean underwear, etc. She said she never was sure what she would be getting, but it was fun to be surprised. For her, it was just another step in faith. It was also the only way she could have afforded to make the 2,700 mile journey.

After meeting dozens of young thru hikers, I better understood that one of the many things they had failed to take into consideration about hiking the PCT was its substantial financial toll. Given my six weeks on the Washington section of the PCT and extrapolating that to a thru hiker's three to four months on the trail, the cost of hiking the entire Trail had to be somewhere between 3,000 and 4,000 dollars. And that wasn't counting the price of transportation if that person traveled from out of state. Hiking the PCT was not a cheap undertaking.

I built up the fire as she started sorting through her backpack to gather what she needed to fix dinner. We talked as she prepared her meal, and I thought that I rarely had met anyone who used the word "awesome" more than she. It started to grind on my nerves when we heard another voice coming out of the darkness. Within seconds, another person hiking in the dark of night came into the campsite and asked to join us. "*Mi casa, su casa,*" was my typical response to such a request. If there were any spot that another tent could get pitched, a person was always welcome to stay.

The new arrival was from Stuttgart, Germany. He had come to the States for the second time in the past three years. Two years ago he had hiked the Appalachian Trail and returned this year to hike the PCT. The two had met up from time to time over the past couple of months, so they had a lot of catching up to do. I wanted to get to bed, so I excused myself, invited them to use up all the wood they needed, and I headed to my tent. It was another one of those chance encounters along the trail that brought more depth and substance to my days alone.

The only problem with the entire meeting was that they remained by the fire for the next couple hours, chatting it up, and I couldn't get to sleep. My tent was less than fifteen feet away, and it wasn't as though the material was soundproof. And I wasn't going to play "dorm daddy" and tell them to quiet down and go to bed. But, what the hell, it was my campsite and they could have been a little more respectful! It reminded me of when I was traveling in Europe in my youth. The rudest and most obnoxious people whenever I stayed at a youth hostel were typically the Germans, closely followed by the Australians. I lay in my sleeping bag with those memories I hadn't thought about in over forty years.

***

One afternoon in midsummer, 1962, I called Bob and asked if he'd quit college, hitchhike across the U.S., and spend a year together traveling in Europe and several points beyond. With hardly a pause, he agreed. We began the drill of attending to all the details for our upcoming adventure. Among the most difficult was informing our parents. His mother and father were livid but soon became resigned. My mother was ecstatic and encouraging, saying that if I didn't do it now, I would probably never do it. My college coach was furious and threatened that if, or when, I returned, I would not be welcomed back on the track team. Friends were mixed. Some prophesied that once I quit, I would never return. Others chimed in with more encouraging comments.

For as much as I would later distance myself from my mother, for a variety of reasons, her encouragement, which I took to be her permission, was probably the greatest gift she ever gave me. Sadly, I was too stubborn and waited too late to tell her. Both Bob and I returned to college and eventually completed respective graduate programs. Many of the naysayers never did travel to Europe.

***

I met Bob when we were fourteen and freshmen in high school. It was immediate attraction and we remained close friends and buddies for over fifty years until his death three years ago. Our friendship lasted through all the turbulence of adolescence: garden-variety high school drama, girlfriends, double dating, pranks played on other friends (and non-friends), sports teams (he was pure brawn and football, I was tall, skinny, and into cross-country and track), surfing at Southern California beaches, dealing with equally crazy parents, years of college, first jobs, first wives, first mortgages, second wives, second mortgages, second families, and all the physical and emotional challenges that the ensuing years brought. Through it all, we remained friends and confidants, and seldom did two weeks pass when one of us didn't pick up the phone and contact the other. I think we both sensed our friendship was a rare commodity in a throwaway world of caprice and neglect.

After high school, Bob stayed near home while I ventured north to Washington. He attended a large State university and I attended a small Northwestern private college. He played football and I ran cross-country and track. But after our sophomore year, we began our adventures in Europe, most of the Near and Middle Eastern countries, Northern Africa. Then it was back home across the Atlantic Ocean to pick up where we had left: college, sports, girlfriends, choices for graduate schools, and dreams for bright and promising careers.

***

It was while lying in my tent listening to the Truly Annoying Mr. Stuttgart and the saccharin Ms. Awesome Christian that I began to recall memories dormant for over forty years.

After several weeks of hitchhiking and for some forgotten, unfathomable reason, Bob and I decided to purchase a used Isetta, and rather than travel by rail or hitchhiking, we would have our own transportation. We would drive this tiny, two-person, front-loading vehicle throughout Germany, over the Swiss and Yugoslavian Alps, into other Balkan countries, and eventually throughout other countries as we made our way to Israel. Of course, in our magical, adolescent thinking, we never considered what we would do if the thing broke down, where we'd get the money for repairs, the various convoluted processes we would have to confront regarding permits and insurances as we entered other countries with a vehicle registered in Germany to two Americans. But we did manage to drive it to Vienna, where we had a wild time driving around that ancient, magnificent city.

I met Maria the second day we arrived in Vienna while staying at a youth hostel. Maria was a Flemish woman in her mid-twenties "on holidays" from Antwerp, Belgium. We met in the lobby one evening and I invited her to play chess with me in the lounge, since the heavy winter snows of the past several days made traveling and sightseeing nearly impossible. So, for the next few days, Bob, Maria, and I hung out together and made short walking excursions to nearby shops and cafes that were accessible from the hostel. Maria was strikingly pretty, cultured, playful, and, best of all, she was multilingual. She seemed to enjoy the attention of the two young Americans with our naïve sense of the world, our bravado to enter places where we barely understood a word being spoken, and living each day as it came with no particular plan or vision for the morrow.

We three became an item, and when the streets became safer to travel, we spent our days together discovering Vienna as a threesome. Bob and I provided the transportation, the funds, the American swagger and humor, and Maria was our translator, our beautiful companion, and our exotic new friend. It was a grand and successful week, and downtown Vienna became a familiar destination and place to spend a day.

On the last evening before Maria had to catch a train to return home, we all stuffed ourselves into the tiny Isetta and headed off to find an opera to attend. Memory doesn't serve me how or where, but we got tickets to see Mozart's *The Magic Flute*. But we did and Maria and I were enthralled and delighted; Bob slept through its entirety.

On our way home to the hostel, we took a wrong turn and found ourselves headed in the wrong direction on a one-way street. Things wouldn't have been so bad except for the fact that down the middle of the street were tracks that were about a foot lower than the street surface itself. In seconds we saw the lights of the streetcar coming our way about two hundred yards from us. Bob was driving, and as we realized what was going on, he attempted to steer the car from one side of the street to the other, and in so doing, this tiny automobile plunked itself right down into the track grooves where our tires got immediately wedged. The streetcar kept coming towards us. We jumped out of the car and began waving furiously at the moving streetcar, yelling at the conductor to stop. Then, simultaneously, we all burst into laughter that practically immobilized us.

The conductor saw the problem: two crazy men screaming, frantically jumping up and down, and laughing while a tiny car was wedged into the tracks. Maria was standing off to one side watching this entire comedic drama, and who knows what was going on in her mind. So Bob and I did what any two sensible young men would do when their car was stuck between two rails in the middle of a street in Vienna: We counted to three, hoisted the thing out off the tracks, put it back on the street, yelled at Maria to "get in," crammed ourselves back into position, and took off down the street towards the hostel laughing so hard Bob could barely see to drive straight. Over the span of many years, Bob and I still laughed about that incident, and if both of us weren't telling it together, no one would have believed it actually occurred. But it did, and it was one among many fond memories of our long friendship.

The next morning, Maria left for Antwerp. Just before she caught the bus to the train station, she presented me with a gift for my twenty-first birthday. It was a recorder, and over the next dozen or so years, I taught myself pieces especially written for that instrument. But somewhere amidst the stops and turns in my life, I lost that precious gift.

That morning, Maria and I exchanged addresses, and soon upon returning home, I wrote her a four-page typed letter. Several months later the envelope was stamped "return to sender." Maria had my address but never wrote, and from time to time over the next several years I would wonder whatever became of her. I suppose some things can never be recreated.

Bob left Vienna to join up with some girl he'd met in Poland. I couldn't remember anyone he'd met in Poland, but off he went, driving our goofy two-person car. I left Vienna a day later with two women from France headed for Gratz. My destination was Istanbul. I soon discovered it was easier to hitchhike with young, attractive women than alone. Two months later, Bob and I met up in Jerusalem, where I was working in a kibbutz somewhere in the Sea of Galilee district.

Years after we returned to the States, after Bob had completed law school and I had finished seminary and we were deep into our respective careers, he received a notice from the Yugoslavian government demanding payment for some outrageous fine for the cost of their disposing of an Isetta registered in his name. Apparently it had been discovered at the bottom of a ravine several hundred feet down the side of a mountain. Bob claimed he knew nothing about our shitty little car being pushed off the side of a cliff or why he arrived in Israel minus the Isetta.

***

Bob wasn't much of a backpacker. I think he wanted to be, but as the years ensued, he took less and less care of his health and gained an enormous amount of weight. I also believe the remnants of injuries from years of being slammed about as a linebacker both in high school and college had done untold damage. I think it was his knees that were the most troublesome, so carrying a pack and moving his large body up and down trails, over boulders, and tree stumps was painful. But being who he was, Bob consented to travel up to the Northwest on several occasions to backpack with me and a couple of my friends. The last backpack we took together was into the area of Hurricane Ridge. But on the first day of hiking, Bob fell and landed on his most damaged knee, so the next several days were pure agony for him. I remember how annoyed I felt that he'd let himself get so out of shape. I think I was more worried than annoyed but didn't know how to express it. What Bob probably experienced from me was annoyance rather than the fear that I might lose my best friend. He was fifty, dangerously overweight, and looked and walked like a fat old man. I should have said something to him. But I didn't. It was soon after that experience that Bob had his first stroke. It was a minor one, but it was the beginning of a long and arduous journey of other health and personal problems: loss of cognitive skills, loss of his fourth marriage, loss of income, loss of mobility, loss of a future that promised anything but more of the same.

I was selfish. I wanted my friend Bob to be well. I wanted his sharp wit, wicked humor, quick retorts, and his loud, infectious laugh to return. I wanted him to backpack with me into our future, and I wanted us to be very old men together laughing and indulging in memories of our life-long friendship. But Bob died three years ago. He had suffered his last and most damaging stroke and could no longer speak or organize his world with any clarity or certainty. My strong, independent, fearless friend had become a dependent, immobile, incontinent man who lived his last years in a small room in a nursing home surrounded by strangers. He died one morning with an aide by his side. To my knowledge, his two daughters from his third marriage never came to visit or say their final goodbyes, though I doubt that Bob would have even noticed. None of his ex-wives came to visit, and aside from his two adult sons from his second marriage, I was the only friend or colleague who came to sit by his side, hold his hand, and express fondness and friendship.

When I flew to Los Angeles to visit Bob for the last time, I brought pictures of us on one of our backpacks, along with a few pictures from earlier years together. It took him about a half a minute of intense peering, but he finally smiled, so I knew he knew what they meant.

I held his hand on that last, late morning of our visit and told him he was the best friend I had ever had, that I had loved him most all of my life, and that I would miss him every day for its remainder. He squeezed my hand, so I think he understood this would be our last meeting. After a few minutes, I rose, bent over, and kissed his bald head. When I looked down at him, tears were streaming down his checks. I buried my head into his neck and cried for a few minutes. I wanted to grow old with Bob. Now I was telling him goodbye for the last time. I had thought that because of his decency and goodness and life of generosity he would be protected. I hoped for a miracle.

Three weeks later I called the assisted living home to ask how Bob was doing and they told me he had died in his sleep the previous night. One of his sons sent me his ashes.

Years earlier, during one of our backpacks as we sat on the ledge of a boulder that jutted out into space overlooking a colorful, spacious, and glorious Spider Meadow in the Cascade Mountain Range, he asked me to spread his ashes in the valley below. I grunted and complained that it was a hell of a hike to get there and kidded him that I would rather go down to the ocean near my house and spread them on the water. He wouldn't have any of it. He wanted his ashes to float down the side of the mountain into that gorgeous valley or he would, in his own words, "come back to haunt me."

Bob's ashes are still packed in a small wood box safely placed on a shelf above my workbench in the garage. In the end, the weight of my friend is less than two pounds.

While I lay in my tent listening to the chattering couple, I promised myself I would hike up to the place where he asked that I spread his ashes. It wouldn't be this year, but maybe the next. I thought that I better get to it because my own knees and feet were starting to fail me and I wasn't sure how many more summers I would be hiking into the wilderness.

Memories of Bob are bittersweet. A person doesn't get that many "best friends" in his life. He would either have to be an exceptional person or very lucky. I am neither, and that is why I understood that Bob's nearly sixty-year friendship was a rare and genuine gift.

***

A person might assume that because of the staggering amount of energy expended every day for eight to twelve hours of hiking, I would just fall exhausted into my tent every night and be in REM sleep within minutes. Not so. That was rarely the case. I think my body just wouldn't shut down. And my feet hurt so damned much, their pain alone would often keep me from sleeping. But, as it turned out, I was in good company. Most the hikers I met experienced the same condition. And it wasn't the discomfort of sleeping on the ground. I had an adequate sleeping pad that provided a level of soft comfort. I just couldn't get seven or eight hours of sleep. So it felt that every day I began with sleep deprivation. I think that's why a zero day from time to time was important. It allowed my body to take a needed break. It gave me an opportunity to catch a few "cat naps," and it got me off my sore feet.

On Day Twenty-Nine, as the first hint of light showed, I stayed in my warm sleeping bag and purposely waited until I knew that Ms. Awesome Christian and the Truly Annoying Mr. Stuttgart had left before I unzipped my tent and stumbled out into the crisp, clear morning air. I say, "stumbled," because most mornings my body was achy and stiff. I was barely halfway through the hike and I was already weary of the hard ground and thin sleeping pad. I ached, literally, for a real bed with a decent mattress. The good news was that the bugs that had swarmed around me the previous night had yet to show. So, my sore back notwithstanding, I considered myself fortunate to begin the day without chatty people or annoying gnats. I wasn't sure which was worse.

Deep Lake lay at 4,500 feet of elevation, and my plan was to hike the three miles to the top of Cathedral Pass at 5,600 feet by midmorning. It would be a challenging climb and a beautiful one.

The embers of the fire from the previous night were still glowing, so I gathered the hottest ones into a small pile and placed several smaller twigs on top to start a fire for some warmth in the morning crispness. Stevens Pass was thirty miles from where I sat and I knew I couldn't make it in one day, as last night's camping companions planned.

From Deep Lake to Stevens Pass was a series of steep trails and switchbacks. That distance would probably take me two and a half days. I was already a day behind the time I had told Carla I would be arriving at Stevens Pass for my next reload box. So, in the face of that reality, I did what any sensible person would do. I lingered even longer by the warm fire, drank another cup of awful instant coffee, and simply enjoyed the peace of the early morning.

I had packed a small New Testament in my gear that included the Psalms, so I often began mornings with a moment of meditation over one of them. I sat by the fire, sipped my coffee, and read from my Bible. I wanted to begin every day in this manner, but some mornings I was so intent on getting on the trail that I abandoned my best-laid plans for a few extra minutes of hiking. In retrospect, that choice seems pretty silly.

A little before 8:00 a.m., I was packed and ready. Like every morning before leaving a campsite, I circled around the area where I had camped to assure myself that I hadn't left anything behind or any trace of my being there. If possible, I spread out the ashes on the ground, cleaned up remnants of wood I had collected the previous night, and on my way out of the area looked back to assure myself that the campsite was fit for the next person. This is a routine I had established for all my years of backpacking. As a young boy, learning to survey a campsite before departing was a lesson learned from Don and Glenn. I do it now almost as a reflex, but that particular morning I thought again about its genesis and said a quiet thanks towards the heavens for all the kindness, instruction, and patience those two men showed towards me during my first few years in the mountains. Little would they ever know that what they taught me remained indelible.

The trail led me around the lake that was calm in the early morning. There was a blanket of morning haze over the water, and I didn't spot anyone who had camped there during the night. The two other campers who joined me the previous night and I were the only ones at the lake.

Because the morning was so crisp, I had kept my thermo clothes on, but two miles into the day, my body had sufficiently warmed. I stopped to peel off one of the layers. The place where I stopped was an opening along the switchback and a place where I could look down the mountain and see Deep Lake two miles away. I spotted no other campers and the lake sat calm and beautiful in the valley below. To my immediate right, I could see the majestic peak of Mt. Stuart and the glistening snow that remained on its slopes. In the distance I could hear the muted sound of a waterfall, though I couldn't see it from where I sat. With the thermo clothes packed away, I remained seated on a rock and simply stared at all the beauty before me. I thought how easy it would be to sit in that very place for the entire day.

Journal Entry:

If Bob were here, he'd probably change his mind and want me to toss his ashes off this ledge. I'd put my foot down on that request! This would be a bitch to return to.

I miss Carla this morning. I wonder who's preaching, and if she went to church or just stayed in bed, read the paper, had a second cup of coffee, then slipped back into needed slumber.

I hope the latter.

I like the fact that I can sit right here and not have to answer to someone else's request to "get going." I can set my own pace...which thus far this morning is akin to a snail's pace.

I'd better get to Stevens Pass pretty soon because I just used my last bit of TP. Who would have thought that something that non-consequential could make a big difference in the peace of mind of a long-distance backpacker? I have no TP! What to do? What to do?

24

—TO PASS

It seemed appropriate that on a Sunday morning I climbed a steep switchback towards Cathedral Pass. It added a sort of Dante-esque metaphor to my own journey of faith over a lifetime of starts and stops and starts again. Faith never came naturally for me. It seemed that most of my "believing" friends didn't struggle to maintain their faith. I, on the other hand, struggled each step of the way. Or perhaps they did struggle but just weren't willing to own up to their own doubts. I often felt like an imposter, as if I were the emperor with no clothes and everyone around me was in denial. There were long stretches of time when I didn't even darken the door of a church, let alone give much thought to a personal faith or a relationship to God. In those times, I was the proverbial Prodigal Son. I had taken my inheritance and stumbled around in one wilderness after another only to squander it all.

Even as a student at Princeton Seminary, I often felt out of place, as if I were pretending to be someone I wasn't but didn't know what to do about it so just muddled through from class to class, one exam to another, week to week, month to month, until I graduated after three years. I never actually lied about possessing a belief in God. I just skirted the question altogether. I simply posed as someone with a plethora of questions seeking deeper understanding. That was a mixture of truth and bullshit. Most of the time, I felt like an imposter with nothing else to do with my life at that time, so I stuck with the program, learned just enough Greek, Hebrew, and Latin for required translations, and studied the courses required. When I felt I was becoming more and more adrift at the seminary, I would head off to the philosophy department at the university and matriculate in their classes or read piles of books that never made it on the required reading lists. So it was no great surprise to anyone that, upon my graduation from Princeton, I was not ordained and didn't begin a pastoral ministry. I remained the Prodigal Son with a seminary degree.

I don't know when or how or where I finally came around to a renewed or a resurgence of faith. I don't think it was any one moment or thing or experience. I suppose one could say that the Spirit does move and work uniquely with each person. My own re-conversion was a gradual and tentative experience. And I think it was more about giving up and acceptance than a particular struggle to get to any one place in the continuum of believing. I suppose it was something akin to Pascal's Wager: I had more to gain than lose by accepting God and believing in His presence, whether in my small, finite life or in the vast cosmos. I simply surrendered. Maybe I came to an undisclosed juncture where I tired of celebrating my doubts and yearned for something beyond the emptiness of cynicism.

Ultimately, I did proceed through all the ordination processes, accepted pastoral positions, and generally made my peace with God, as I understood Him. I left the pastoral ministry a long time ago but still remained active in various churches wherever I could, but there remains in me, still, a grain of caution and doubt. Most doctrines I have no patience for, and a lot of what organized religion is about drives me shit-batty. But I am no longer willing to "throw the babe out with the bathwater."

Sometimes I miss the life of being a pastor and the opportunities that position afforded me. But it comes with too dear a price to pay, and I no longer have the patience or willingness to subject myself, or my family, to such scrutiny and accountability of thought, language, and lifestyle. I have, what I like to claim, a workable faith. If nothing else, it is an honest faith and I don't have to pose as someone I am not. In the final analysis, there is something to be said about integrity. I believe what I am able to accept as my own truth. The mustard seed of faith that I possess is sufficient for my life, and, best of all, I know that God accepts me as I am, warts and all.

***

By the evening of Day Twenty-Nine, I had only hiked around eleven miles, a day of difficult switchbacks and drastic elevation climbs and descents. I found a small campsite at Deception Pass, and again, the first order of business was to remove my boots and socks, put on my Tevas, and boil some water for tea. And, horror of horrors, I used the last of my sugar. And it was buggy as hell again. I had hiked all day without even a hint of a bug anywhere around me, but the second I sat to relax at the end of the day, they found me. I had long since stopped using any bug repellent. In fact, I may have just tossed it at the last stop. No matter how much I used or how thick I spread it over my exposed skin, I got no results. It just felt sticky and smelly, and when I crawled into my sleeping bag at the end of the day it just rubbed off on the material. Experience informed me that the most effective deterrent was campfire smoke or cigar smoke, but I had smoked my last cigar at the Deep Lake campsite. So I sipped my tea and for the remainder of the evening swatted bugs.

Like most nights, I camped alone and headed to bed early. Except for the breeze through the trees surrounding my tent, there was silence. I was grateful for the solitude.

My plan had been to arrive at Stevens Pass by Saturday or, at the very least, by Sunday so Carla could drive up to meet me with my new pack and other provisions for the next leg of the hike. Also, I had not seen her since we parted at the trailhead just beyond the Bridge of the Gods over four weeks prior. But hard as I tried, I simply could not make the miles work in our favor. It was a huge disappointment. Even so, I still wanted to get on the trail as early as possible on Day Thirty to at least guarantee I wouldn't fall further behind in my roughly outlined schedule. So, by 7:00 a.m., I was hiking. My left big toenail ached as though it were getting infected. With nearly every step, it felt as though an ice pick were being stabbed through the nail. My God, it hurt! But forward was my only option, so forward I kept hiking, and again, the day was all about going up and up across several more switchbacks.

I was halfway up the switchback towards Pieper Pass at about 6,000 feet elevation when I stopped to catch my breath, which I seemed to be doing more and more during the day. It was hot and there was little shade cover on the trail hiking up the side of the mountain. There were no obstructions as far as the eye could see, so I dropped The Rock next to where I stood, looked through my pack to find the cell phone Carla had sent in my reload box at Snoqualmie Pass, and dialed her work number on the remote possibility there was sufficient clearance for a call to connect. And behold, there was!

Carla answered immediately, and before I could barely get a sentence out of my mouth, I burst into tears. Perhaps out of sheer exhaustion, perhaps the feeling of accomplishment and being in the midst of such largeness, maybe it was just hearing her voice. She was baffled and kept asking if I was alright, was I hurt, had something happened.

"No," I managed to blurt. I quickly gathered my wits. "I took the chance that I could get through to you. I'm okay. Just tired and a day behind schedule, so we won't be able to meet at Stevens Pass."

Her voice was calm and assured me it was okay to be a few days late and that she would figure out how to get my new pack and reload box to me. The connection kept crackling in and out, so I said a hurried goodbye and turned off the phone. I stood in the middle of the trail looking up to where I had to go to get to the top of Pieper Pass, looked west at the vastness of the Alpine Wilderness, blew my nose, wiped my eyes, hoisted The Rock on my back, and headed up the trail. I felt a little silly thinking that I could barely talk to my own wife, given the emotional outburst, but at least I reached her and she would know I was safe, had not fallen off a cliff, and was not far from Stevens Pass.

***

Journal Entry:
I'm standing at the crest of Pieper Pass at 6,000 feet and enjoying a near 360-degree view of the Alpine Lakes

Wilderness. I've taken off my pack and am sitting on the nearest rock, drinking several long swigs of water from one of my bottles. I slid off the rock onto the dry, dusty ground and splayed my entire body on the dirt. I feel relief to have finished another switchback. But I also feel a deep sense of wonder about all I am experiencing and seeing and encountering.

I can't remember the last time I felt "wonder" about anything. When was the last time when the only response I could conjure was "Wow?" I'm so grateful that, over the course of this trek, I have had many of these moments. I hope for more.

I checked my map and realized that for the next three or four miles I would be descending to around 4,700 feet. Downhill hiking has its drawbacks, as any backpacker will attest, but sometimes a break from the uphill grind of switchbacks has its definite advantages. I lay on the ground for about a half hour before heading down from the pass. I felt refreshed, but I could have easily slept for an hour or so. Carla wouldn't be worried, I was only a day and a half from Stevens Pass, the day was sunny, Glacier Peak stood boldly beautiful in the distance, and I had completed over half of the Washington section of the PCT without any major or harmful incidents. I was feeling pretty satisfied with myself.

***

I had not seen any other hikers since leaving Deep Lake and climbing over Cathedral Pass. But as I hiked closer to Stevens Pass, I began to encounter day hikers heading for Glacier Lake, Trap Lake, Hope Lake, Mig Lake, or Josephine Lake. Even the most out-of-shape hiker could successfully reach one of those lakes. For the first time since I'd left, I had no interest in engaging with any of them. They came in clusters and were noisy, overdressed with too much stuff for a one- or two-day hike, and I was on a mission to get as close to Stevens Pass as possible before ending the day. I did want to stop at Mig Lake for a quick rest around 4:00 p.m., but the sandy area by the lake where I wanted to stop was taken. Eight or so people had managed to drag along two large blow-up mattresses and were sitting by the water smoking and drinking bottles of beer. "Shit!" I murmured under my breath and hiked on.

Five miles north I reached the north shore of Lake Susan Jane. As I approached, I gleefully noticed I was the only person around the lake. It was a small body of water, maybe about ten acres, with ample flat areas for camping and an abundance of accessible dry wood for my evening campfire. I had hiked sixteen miles, was about four miles south of Stevens Pass, and very ready to end the day.

Though there were signs declaring that campfires were illegal, for only the second time since I began the PCT, I ignored cautionary signage and proceeded with common sense. I gathered some wood and built the fire close enough to the lake so if anything went awry I could access the water. I also kept the fire very small and away from any trees. I figured with all the years of Scouting, YMCA camping lessons, and over fifty years of backpacking, I knew how to build and maintain a safe fire. It was a risk, but the evening temperature was falling and my clothes were wet from a day of perspiration. Though I quickly changed into my thermo clothes, a chill was setting into my body. The heat from the fire would be a welcome end of the day. It would also dry my clothes for the following day's hike.

***

Stevens Pass! On the thirty-first day of the adventure that began a few yards northwest of the Bridge of the Gods, I arrived at Stevens Pass after 325 miles of hiking. I was three quarters towards the end, and of all the hiking I had done in my lifetime, this had been the most challenging and taxing.

I left Lake Susan Jane almost at daybreak with only a breakfast bar and a quick cup of coffee for the morning meal before I headed out. I didn't want to spend any extra time cooking. Though it was only a four-mile jaunt to the

Pass, it was a steep hike out of the gorge where I had camped, about a thousand-foot elevation in slightly over a mile. "Steep" would be an understatement. But I was energized by pure enthusiasm to finish this leg of the PCT and meet up with someone, anyone, from home who would bring me my new pack and reload box.

I reached the top of the pass where the turnabouts for the chairlifts were standing in their summer solitude. It was a bit eerie to think that in just a few months where I was standing there would be several feet of packed snow and hundreds of noisy, active, bustling skiers hopping off the chairs to head back down the mountain as swiftly as their courage dared. At that moment, this place was peaceful and belonged only to me. I was in no hurry to rush down the mountain.

It was midmorning and I found a flat rock that faced north so I could sit and look down to where I was about to hike. I had another two miles before finishing this section. I wanted to savor the moment. I found some dry food that was easily accessible, turned on my phone, and dialed my daughter, Paige, to tell her where I was and what I had accomplished. Her phone went immediately to voicemail, and as I began to leave a message, my emotions got the best of me and I started to cry halfway through my message. So I hung up. The honest truth is that I was simply overwhelmed by it all, by the fact I was older than any other person I had met on the trail, that I had managed to hike from the border of Oregon/Washington to the very spot where I was sitting. I had experienced many kindnesses and acts of generosity. I had a family who were supportive and enthused at my willingness to take up this challenge. I was so happy to be sitting at that very spot at that time in my life with a feeling of largeness and gratitude and satisfaction.

I felt something beyond anything I had ever felt before. I felt peace and joy and happiness and relief, all at the same time. I felt full of life. And I felt that my left big toe was going to explode with pain. Nothing like that piece of reality to bring me back to the moment! I still had two miles to reach Highway 2 and a twelve-mile hitchhike down to the tiny settlement of Skykomish. But at that moment, I savored the clear air and the blue sky. Not even the incessant buzzing of the power lines above me could take away the perfection of the moment.

After a half hour or so, I packed my food bag and strapped on The Rock for the two-mile hike down the mountain. The hike to the pass was not an easy one. It was steeper than I had anticipated, and there were lots of loose rocks that needed to be carefully navigated, exposed roots across the trail, and hairpin switchbacks. I kept thinking what a screw up it would be for me to fall now after all those miles and so close to the pass. I crossed several small creeks, where I stopped to fill my water bottles and to wish a couple day hikers a good day of hiking. They were headed for Mig Lake, so weren't interested in any information I could offer. And there wasn't much to offer except for them to keep hiking and enjoy all the lakes and streams and meadows along the way. I bit my tongue to keep from blurting, "And clean up all your shit before you hike out."

Journal Entry:
Hitchhiked to Skykomish (population: 198) and am sitting in the restaurant on the ground floor of the Cascadia Hotel where I have a room for the night. $60.00 and for $5.00 extra bucks they will do my laundry for me! The hotel was built in the early 1920s and has kept its historical charm.

A couple women picked me up along the highway along with another PCTer who was on his way to the Dinsmore's Hiking Haven in the small town of Baring where thru hikers stay for a minimal cost and can hang out and do laundry. I chose the hotel room route. After all the weeks of solitude, I'm not ready for a crowd of people vying for bragging rights.

I called Carla, and Jonah is on his way. Will be arriving around 1:00 or so.

Right now, as I write, an enormous plate of corn beef hash has been set before me, with toast, hash brown spuds, coffee, and fresh-squeezed OJ. I may just sit here for the rest of my life.

Actually, after this meal, I'm headed up to my room and will soak in the bathtub for as long as I can before the raisin effect sets in. It's a funky hotel built for the miners and railroad workers who worked in these parts. I like the feel of it.

Who knows who may have been sitting in this very room in the 20s and 30s, resting their own weary selves? This is nice. What would make it nicer would be for Carla to be sitting across from me admiring my accomplishment.

***

Day Thirty-Two at Skykomish. I decided to take another zero day. My left big toe was so painful I could barely get my foot into the boot. In the scheme of things, one more day of rest didn't put me that far behind. So I opted to wear my sandals in hopes my toe would recover enough for me to proceed.

The day before, Jonah had taken a half day off work and met me at the hotel in the early afternoon. He brought my new pack and the reload box I had packed several weeks before leaving. As usual, Carla had stuffed a few extra goodies into it, along with another note of encouragement: *No one to debrief my life with...miss you, proud of you. Be safe out there and come home in one piece.* I think I looked forward to those notes almost as much as the food and fresh socks. Hell, I could probably buy the food and socks in some town where I stopped, but no amount of money could buy those notes. I kept them all, frayed from being handled by my grubby hands and reread several times over.

We sat at a corner table by the window and ordered lunch. I could look out at the railroad tracks about fifty yards away and watch the Great Northern ease its way west towards Seattle. There was a time when this was a "happen'n" town crowded with miners, lumberjacks, and railroad workers. Now it was just a stopover for groceries and a meal before the skiing crowd drove the dozen miles up Highway 2 to Stevens Pass.

I sat quietly watching my youngest son with the kind of wonder parents have when the epiphany strikes that the person before them has suddenly jumped from the wading pools of childhood into the sea-world of adulthood. While listening to him describe his summer job, his life in the University District living with high school buddies who'd been friends practically since they'd been wearing Pull-Ups, and his plans for the fall when he started back to school, my heart was filled with pride. He was already making plans to spend several months in China at a language institute.

I looked at my youngest son with fascination. I could barely think of him as a man with his own life full of plans and aspirations. I wanted him to stay fixed in time. He had grown up too quickly and too soon for my liking. For himself, he probably hadn't grown up soon enough. We lingered over lunch longer than I thought he would tolerate, but he didn't seem to be in any rush. Jonah has always been the child who would engage and share. Sometimes he revealed a bit more than I wanted to know! He declined the freshly baked pie, but I went full bore and had a big slice of apple pie with ice cream. More than the pie, I just wanted to extend our time together that afternoon.

After lunch we headed up to my room and unpacked the reload box. I emptied out my old pack on the bed and sorted out what I wanted to keep from the box. The next leg of the PCT was a hundred miles, and I needed to keep my pack as light as possible, even despite the extra food required over the eight days it would take. From others I'd met who'd hiked from north to south, and from my guidebooks, I understood this would be the toughest section. I placed the gear I didn't need back in the box to send home with Jonah. I walked him down to his car, gave him a long hug, smiled while he took a "selfie" of us, then moved to the side of the street, watching him drive away, over the bridge, and onto the highway until I couldn't see his car. I walked back to my room and took a nap.

***

On the morning of Day Thirty-Three, I checked out of the hotel even before the restaurant had opened, so I went into the small lounge to have coffee and wait with a couple of others for breakfast. Among them was Sam, whom I had met at Mirror Lake, south of Snoqualmie Pass. He had left the trail to rest a few days before resuming. Now he was with his wife, who had brought his reload box to Skykomish. He asked if I wanted to start the next section with him, but I wanted to get to the trailhead right after breakfast and he wanted to hang around Skykomish with his wife until early afternoon. We said our goodbyes.

I walked the quarter mile from the hotel to the highway and stuck out my thumb to hitch a ride to the trailhead ten miles north. It only took about a hundred yards to realize The Rock was heavier than I wanted, but there was no turning back. Remembering what Carla had told me as I'd begun the first day standing by her car, I would just have to eat my way through the food until the pack got lighter.

Within five minutes, a German family of four stopped, rearranged their own luggage, and made room for me. The wife and husband were both physicians visiting from Munich on their way to Leavenworth with their two teenage children. We had several miles to talk about their experiences in the U.S. and my experiences on the PCT. We competed for whose story was more interesting. The two children were fascinated that this old guy in their rented SUV had been hiking several hundred miles alone in the wilderness. I told them of my positive experiences in Germany and about Bob and me wandering from city to city asking over and over, *"Wo ist eine Jungenheirberge?"* ("Where is a youth hostel?") I swear, between Bob and me, we must have asked that question five hundred times over the course of a few weeks.

At one time in my life, I thought I would write a book about our travels and one of the chapters would definitely be titled: "Where is the Youth Hostel?" But that book never got written and most my memories of Germany have long since faded. The family laughed at my story, or most likely, at my wretched German pronunciation.

At 10:00 a.m., I was finally on the trail headed north towards Stehekin. I had entered the Glacier Peak Wilderness, which, along with the John Muir Trail in the California High Sierras, is considered the most challenging yet beautiful hiking anywhere in the U.S. Though it was another one hundred miles to Stehekin and my next and last reload box, for the first time since I'd begun the hike, I felt ready to finish. My pack was loaded with about eight days' worth of food, there was a stabbing pain in my lower back, and my left toe was killing me. Basically, I was worn out about a hundred fifty miles before the finish. It was a thought I dared not ponder with too much intensity.

During the next few miles, I thought a lot about the several thru hikers I had met over the course of my own trek. I admitted to a renewed respect and awe for their commitment and toughness. To maintain several months of intensity and perseverance was beyond anything I had accomplished. They started on the Mexico/California border and headed north for 2,700 miles. I did hear various figures about the rate of attrition, but even so, those who kept on were an amazing group.

Within a few miles I came to Nason Creek and, with its perfect campsites, was tempted to stop for the day. But I resisted and hiked down to Lake Valhalla for a late lunch. There, I met a young couple who had stopped for an afternoon respite on their way to Skykomish. They had started at Harts Pass with the Columbia Gorge as their destination. I got an earful of all the hazards that awaited me over the next several days: rushing streams, washed-out bridges, treacherous and ill-kept trails, and on and on. I could feel my heart race with anxiety. I even considered heading back to Skykomish and ending my trek. With a painful toe and a heavy pack, I wasn't certain I was up for the challenge. But pride and stubbornness prevailed, and I talked myself into hoisting The Rock back on and heading another six miles to Lake Janus.

For the next few hours, it was difficult not to focus and worry about all the comments made by the couple I had met at Lake Valhalla. I needed to stay positive and take each mile, each hour, each day as it came to me, and not as others had experienced it. I couldn't allow someone else to define my own experience, even if they were similar. Should they be accurate, I absolutely was not going to quit out of fear. Besides, I believed that, from time to time, it was important to do something that scared me. Fear is not always a bad thing. Being careless, being sloppy, being inattentive is never sensible when in the wilderness. But being a little fearful can open one's senses and challenge some of what we forget we internally possess. So, in a mild state of angst, I trudged on with my sore toe and heavy pack.

I hiked the six miles to Lake Janus alone. The two zero days at Skykomish had been bliss, and the various conversations with other hikers as well as my own son were enjoyable and meaningful. But all the chatter had begun to annoy me, so it felt right and good to be silent again.

The lake was shallow and warm, so before I readied my campsite, I stripped down to total nakedness and waded into the water. That morning I had taken a long bath before checking out of the hotel, so this wasn't a bathing moment. It was simply another skinny-dipping experience in a mountain lake with no other person around to witness or complain. I knew such experiences would soon be in my past rather than my future. I was going to enjoy them when and where I could.

I climbed out of the lake and sat on the nearest rock. The water dripped off my body. The late afternoon warmth of the sun would dry me sufficiently, though right then I didn't want to put anything on. Nakedness seemed appropriate. It was as though I had returned to a time of innocence as I sat in this Eden observing the work of God. But soon enough the sun would slip behind the peaks, dropping the temperature several degrees, so I pulled out my thermo clothes from the bottom of my pack and dressed. I set up my tent, boiled some water for tea, found a perfect place to sit by the edge of the water, then lit up one of the cigars I had purchased in Skykomish. The only sounds I could hear were the lapping of the water on the shore, the chirping of distant birds, and me puffing on the cigar. No one was in sight, the evening was calm and peaceful, and, aside from the German family I had met in the morning, I had spent another day alone in peace.

25

THE NECESSITY OF SOLITUDE

I didn't simply stumble onto solitude. It didn't suddenly occur as if I had come around a sharp corner on the trail and happened upon it. Solitude was intentional. I chose to spend that time in the wilderness solo hiking, though I did encounter many kind and interesting people along the way.

Somewhere among the vastness of his writings, Rilke tells us to love our solitude. I don't think I ever loved the solitude as I hiked the PCT, but I did grow to honor it and see it as a blessing. It is no secret that we live in a culture starved for quiet and silence and privacy. There is precious little of it any longer. And I needed to experience being alone. Hiking with others would mean conversation, and in an odd sort of way, I would not belong to myself. I needed to not require conversation about all the beauty and grandeur that surrounded me every day. So each day I embraced the quiet. Yet even being alone didn't guarantee silence and peace. My head was often filled with the noise of chatter, but I like to think that from time to time I was able to turn it off and listen to the quiet voice of God.

There is a time for everything under heaven. So claims the Old Testament preacher. That evening, on Day Thirty-Three, as I sat on a flat, comfortable rock, chewing on a power bar by the shore of Lake Janus, those words came to mind. Words passed on through thousands of years of oral and written tradition to remind me after a long day of hiking, staring out at the calm surface of a lake, that there is a season for all things, that "there is a time to speak and a time to be silent."

The experience of hiking the PCT was my season of silence, more or less. It was certainly a time for me to be more intentional about daily quiet and reflection. I didn't need to emulate Thoreau or retreat to an ashram in India or join an obscure monastery to experience solitude. The trail itself offered all the raw material necessary. On many days, it was right to remain silent, watch, and listen.

Typically, I talk too much and too often about too many things. Most people do. Loquacious, verbose, chatty have been some of the more generous adjectives to describe me. And sometimes during one or more of my longest days of hiking I thought it may be a colossal cosmic trick that I didn't even come to the wilderness to see one more mountain or cross another stream or camp in yet another peaceful meadow—though all that was wonderful. Maybe this was all about my coming to an understanding that, while I was talking rather than paying attention, my life had gone so quickly from twenty to seventy and to catch a glimpse that life was shorter than I had ever envisioned and there was precious little that remained. Maybe I *was* "almost there." Maybe I was in this very place and time to understand that I would be given a moment of insight that would lead to a profound and permanent insight about the preciousness of life's peaks and valleys.

John Muir knew this when he wrote about the "necessity of the wild"—that there was, in our very DNA, the call to be reconnected with the wilderness. It was in these moments of solitude that I thought about that reconnection, what meaning it has had in my past, and what it could mean in my future.

***

There have been few opportunities in my life for long stretches of silence, few times to be present in uncomplicated and unadulterated beauty and reflect on my past, present, and future. Simply put, there was little extended solitude. Being raised by an Irish-Calvinist mother who had no patience for slackers, she never would have tolerated such a thing as sitting and doing nothing. "Idleness gives opportunity for the devil," she might intone, though I know for certain my mother never believed in any devil. And though she had long passed, I hoped that if she knew of my PCT experience, she'd approve. She'd be a bit baffled by such an endeavor, but I think she'd acknowledge that her son had accomplished something remarkable. I like to think as much.

***

When I returned home from hiking the PCT and returned to the normal routines of my daily life, I often was asked what I did every day. I said I hiked, thought, sang, read, wrote in my journal, and talked with whoever was around.

"And what did you think about and who did you talk to?"

"I talked out loud to myself. I thought about my life, where I had been, the people I had known, the places I had traveled, the people I needed to tell I loved them, the places I wanted to visit or return to, the amends I wanted to make to those I had harmed, you know, those sorts of things."

And they'd respond, "Man, I could never spend all that time alone."

"Sure you could. You simply do it. You get into a rhythm and pretty soon you wonder how you spent so many years not being silent, not pondering your life, not listening to the silences rather than filling every space with chatter."

"And you actually sing and talk to yourself?"

I laughed and shook my head. "Yes. Try it some time. Listen to yourself form words and phrases and sometimes you will notice something interesting coming out of your mouth. And when you sing to yourself during a day of hiking, you don't even have to sing on key. No one is listening or judging. It's quite freeing."

"I just can't imagine an entire day without someone to talk to."

"Then hiking a few hundred miles alone is probably not something you'd enjoy doing."

And that would end that conversation.

I am not entirely new to solitude, but this experience on the PCT was my longest stretch of living in my own isolation from the busy world of human activity. Earlier experiences of solitude prepared me. Beginning in my late twenties, long-distance running took me out of my busy professional, family, and social commitments to hours of quiet discipline. Yes, there were periods in my running experience when I enjoyed the company of running partners to share the long hours of running. But mostly I chose to run alone. It was a time to listen to my body, to have long conversations with myself, and even to resolve some conflict that had been an ongoing annoyance. But I had experiences of being alone and into myself at a much earlier age. It came through my experiences through the world of music.

From around age seven to the end of my teens, I spent hours sitting on a hard, unforgiving bench practicing the piano. By choice. I was one of those rare kids who seldom needed to be reminded to practice. Day after day, years following years, I would practice for hours at a time, often imagining I was a famous concert artist just completing a difficult concerto. Even though I was years away from ever tackling such a challenging piece of music, I spent hours daydreaming that someday I would play with a famous orchestra in front of an large audience of admirers.

When I was twelve years old, I performed a recital with another advanced student of my teacher. She was a stunning fourteen-year-old and played beautifully. That day, I played several pieces of Chopin and Debussy, and she played Brahms and Schubert. About halfway through the program, we played a duet by Grieg. She was dressed in a low-cut formal gown, and the sweet smell of lavender filled the space. It was all very distracting and I could barely concentrate on my part. Our performance was well received, but we didn't play together again until two years later when she was a high school senior and I was a sophomore. She had grown into an even more stunning young woman as I was attempting to maneuver my way through the thorny pathways of puberty, hormones, and various competing distractions. That night we played a two-piano duet of the first movement of Grieg's Piano Concerto, and she still had that faint smell of lavender about her. My fantasy was that the two of us would go into the future together playing duets to the sound of thunderous applauses.

At my twentieth year high school reunion, I asked someone if they knew what had become of Valerie, and it was then I learned that soon after college she had died from a rare and aggressive cancer. To this day, a whiff of lavender can snap me back into those poignant moments. I wonder if, even up to the time of her death, she played with the same depth and passion as I remembered.

All through middle school and high school, I was enlisted to perform at some function or another in the community or in school or church. I always accepted, even though it meant more practice and the balancing of an already crazy schedule. But it brought me a certain level of attention and acclaim that every teenager seeks. And I simply enjoyed playing the piano for people and watching them respond to my performances.

I am still not certain why I abandoned something so personal and meaningful in my life. There are times when I wonder what my life would have been had I remained faithful to my gift and to the discipline of practicing and performing. Yet, even then, while I realized I was very good, I also knew I was not truly exceptional or gifted. To be a respected performer, a person has to be more than very good. At least, I thought that was so then. Now I think, had I received better counsel, I might have reconciled myself to achieving what I could, made peace with possibly being a "good enough" pianist, and grown into my highest level of talent and ability. A kind priest once said to me that the greatest sin we can commit in our lives is to not honor the gifts God gives us.

Over the course of my life, I have wondered, had my father lived, would he have held my feet to the fire and challenged me to face all my dread of confidence, take the risks, and forge ahead to honor my gift. It is one of life's truisms that we cannot change the past, but I do sometimes wonder if I had that part of my life to live over, would I have had the courage to see how far I could have gone. As it happened, I got distracted, and other avenues opened for me to follow. Yet all those early lessons of practicing and attention to detail and memorizing and preparation were profoundly valuable. I learned that to rise to a high level of competency in an instrument (or any endeavor) was not accomplished by committee or bullshitting at the water cooler. It was a solitary and sometimes lonely task. And very early in my life, I embraced it.

By choosing to solo hike the PCT, I chose solitude. And though I spent most of my time on the PCT alone, I was not lonely.

In the end, that time of solitude forced me to think about my priorities and outlook and how I had lived my life. It allowed me time and opportunity to look beyond the immediate. In my experience of solitude, I came to understand that trust and healing were at the heart of any peace I might come to experience.

26

ALMOST THERE

It was the first day of September, and I was feeling a little impressed with myself. I had been hiking over thirty days, ten to twelve hours every day, and covered nearly five hundred miles. I had met some amazing people whose generosity and kindness were humbling, and I had my new pack that REI had switched out for me simply on my word over the phone. Aside from my blindingly painful left big toe and assorted blisters, I was in relatively good shape, and though I had lost several pounds, I felt stronger by the day. Nevertheless, a true confession would reveal that there were many nights I awoke from the pain I was feeling somewhere on/in my body. At those times I would simply lie still and wait until it passed and try to fall back to sleep.

I began this new month with a sense of contentment I had rarely known. I sat by Sitkum Creek sipping coffee, writing a few sentences in my journal, and chewing on a breakfast bar. It was crumbly and stale, but I washed it down with sips of coffee and opened another. I would need the calories for the day's hike. I wanted to make Dolly Vista campsite about sixteen miles away from where I sat. The terrain was as rugged as I had yet encountered, so it would be a long and difficult day of hiking. I started at 3,800 feet of elevation and would reach 5,800 feet by the end of the day. That meant an entire day of ups and downs and multiple switchbacks. Demanding, yes, but the views were glorious beyond description, which helped my aesthetic spirit prod my weary body into moving forward.

About seven miles into the day, I met a man sitting by the side of the trail with his teenage son. They had started in Stehekin and were heading south to Stevens Pass. They had taken the three-hour boat ride from the town of Chelan up the lake to where the trailhead began.

The man invited me to join them, so I dropped my pack and sat awhile. Our conversation led from one thing to another and eventually to the telling about his childhood in India where his father had been the tailor in their small village supporting a family of eight children. His mother didn't work outside the home and they were poor. Forty years ago, at the age of his son (who was sitting with obvious boredom written across his face), he'd come to America to create a better life: went to college, settled into a career, married, and had a large family. He told me that when he came to America he brought with him all his possessions: the clothes he wore for the trip, an extra shirt, a pair of sandals, a windbreaker, a pair of shorts, assorted toiletries. To this day, it remained a mystery how his family managed to scrape together enough money to pay for his passage. When he became successful, he sent money to bring his entire family to America, where they all thrived and where his parents are buried in a family plot. As he spoke, his tears brimmed. Then, after a short pause, he continued, "Now I am retired, and I have a closet full of clothes, more than I can wear, and a house full of things I rarely pay attention to."

And there, in the presence of his bored son, he told me he was happier when he possessed nothing than he has today. Were it his choice, he would go back to those days. He laughed when he said he was the American success story, but in the end, he succeeded in nothing but collecting more things than he wanted or needed.

"No, my friend, my greatest treasure is my family and my great joy today is that this son is with me here. If you have family and health, you have everything."

By now it was close to lunchtime, so we three continued to sit on the side of the trail and share our food. I had more stuff than them, and the boy smiled broadly when I pulled out a Snickers bar and handed it over to him. The father watched as his son tore off the paper and devoured the candy before he ate the lunch his father had prepared. I detected a sense of sadness in the father as he watched his son. It was as if the father had somehow failed to impart the values he himself had been taught as a child.

I left them sitting by the side of the trail as I continued my own day of hiking with the sense I had been in the presence of an itinerant guru imparting wisdom to whomever would welcome it. I thought of these encounters as gifts spread along my pathway for me to open and explore. It was another example that the best things that happened to me along the trail were not planned. I hoped I could hold to that insight when I returned home.

With The Rock securely strapped on, I gathered up my trekking poles and stood on the path heading north. As I began my first step, I turned around and asked, "About how far to Dolly Vista?"

The man replied, "You're almost there."

"Really? Seems like it'd be farther."

He slowly shook his head and reaffirmed, "Nope, you're almost there."

"Well, enjoy the rest of your day." And then I headed north.

Being "almost there" is an all-too-typical response to enquiries about distance from one point to another. I learned soon enough that what one person considered "almost there" wasn't the same for another. To a twenty-something, five miles was a couple-hour walk. For me, depending on the terrain, it could mean a half day of hiking. Receiving such information from someone half my age was usually not helpful, so at some point during my PCT experience, I stopped asking. "Almost there" is different for each hiker. But then, in a different meaning, heading into my seventy-first year on this earth, "almost there" might be more accurate than I wanted to admit!

Journal Entry

The end of a very long fifteen-mile day. Today I felt every year of being seventy. But at the end of each day, no matter how weary, the taste of ice-cold stream water and being in the midst of all this beauty is an elixir that restores me. But even so, while my brain tells me I am a frisky youth, starting at my toes and working up towards my neck, my body tells me I am old.

And why am I doing this? Because I CAN! Because it is a concrete way to not become invisible, a concrete statement that I do exist, that I am capable and strong and courageous. That will have to be reason enough. Yet I must not lose sight that all this is a gift. Time is as gift. In a twinkling of an eye, everything can change. So, I must be thankful for each day with deep gratitude: for all the beauty, the safe hiking, the people I have met, the Trail Angels who have come into my experience at just the right moment. Ah, yes, and I must not forget all the Trail Magic that has showered upon me at just the right time.

I am pondering the Psalm I just read that claims, "I would have lost hope had I not believed I would see the goodness of the Lord among the land of the living." I have seen it in all the Trail Angels I have met.

There is a gentle breeze coming from the north and I will fall asleep with that sound as the last I hear for the day.

27

REFLECTIONS ON SCARCITY AND ABUNDANCE

From the Columbia Gorge trailhead it took me thirty-nine days to reach Stehekin. About thirty-five were hiking days and the others were zero days to relax, do laundry, shave, shower, and plan for the next leg of the hike.

Sometimes it's still hard to imagine that, for six weeks, everything I needed to survive I carried in a pack on my back. During those weeks there were ample sources of water from streams and lakes, I ate three meals each day, and I slept each night in a safe and comfortable place. During those six weeks I met scores of good and interesting and generous people from every imaginable walk of life. I was blessed by several Trail Angels who I encountered at just the right moment. And I always felt I had enough of everything I needed. Most importantly, I carried within me good memories of my family, friends, and especially of Carla. I possessed a strong faith that I was exactly where I was supposed to be each day, and I believed I had not come to the wilderness to fail, lose my way, or be hurt. But it would be a certain bet that if I told most people back home that I could survive for several weeks on what I could carry on my back, I would encounter their doubt.

Much like the gentleman I met who left his home in India with his sparse possessions, I too possessed only the very minimum of things. It never occurred to me that I didn't have enough or that I had less than I needed or wanted. Aside from including crampons on my equipment list, I could not recall any moment when I said, "Oh hell, I should have brought such and such." The most important things in my life could not be carried in a pack, and my happiest and most remarkable moments thus far along the trail had no relation to anything material. It was living proof of what Martin Luther meant when he claimed that security is the ultimate idol.

One of the conversations that often took place in my head was about all the stuff I possessed back home. I thought about the clothes and books and stuff I owned that I never wore or read or used. And so, I challenged myself that, upon my return, I would sort through all my closets and boxes and shelves and give away the clutter. One of the promises I made to myself was that if I hadn't worn a piece of clothing in the past two years and had no interest in ever wearing it again, it would go into a pile to be given to our local thrift shop. Books that had been in boxes for the past several years would all be given away to one place or another. I was committed to divest myself of stuff I neither wanted nor needed. I wasn't committing myself to a monk's life; I just needed to consider living lighter. The pastor of my church once claimed that he'd never seen a hearse hauling a U-Haul trailer.

***

I was thirty-five miles from Stehekin and about one hundred miles from Harts Pass the morning I left Dolly Vista campground. And that day I hiked about fifteen difficult miles through some of the most beautiful parts of the PCT I had thus experienced. I compared it to some of the areas of the High Sierras I had experienced in my youthful years of backpacking. And to think, we are the only country on this planet that protects so much land for public use and enjoyment.

After a long day of difficult hiking, I found a campsite near Suiattle Pass where I had a clear and unobstructed view of majestic Glacier Peak. This snowcapped volcano dominated the entire horizon. I positioned my tent so I could poke my head out the front opening and let the mountain fill my field of vision. It was breathtaking. I sat on a log near my tent, watched the sun set over the peak, and seldom moved from that spot all evening. I pretended that I was the only person on the mountain and perhaps the first person to have ever sat at that very spot. Was it possible to recover a sense of what Eden must have been like, unspoiled, undamaged?

I wondered how this experience would affect the future me. Would something within me be different from completing this section of the PCT, or would this be just another adventure like others I had experienced? Regardless, I felt a deep sense of satisfaction that I had faced so many challenges—physical and emotional—and struggled to this point of near completion. I was conflicted. I wanted to savor the moment, yet I also wanted to be done, meet up with Carla, and go home. The romance of the Trail was all but gone. I was thinking more about what I wanted to do when I returned home than about what I would see or experience in the next few days on the trail. I was thinking of all the yard work that didn't get done in my absence and what my first project would be to bring it back into order. I knew Carla would not have had the time to attend to the gardens with my level of obsessiveness, and I figured most the container plants would have had a near death experience by the time I returned.

Journal Entry:
A day's hike from Stehekin and for the past few days I've been passed by the last few large groups of the thru hikers on their way to Canada. My God, they are a ragged bunch of men and women! I am still hiking at a somewhat leisurely pace and still satisfied that a fifteen-to-twenty-mile day is sufficient. These hikers, on the other hand, are intensely focused on a rapid pace and long miles each day. For some, a thirty-mile day is normal. They will stop in Stehekin for their last reload box, rest for one day, then head towards Manning Park about eight miles across the Canadian border. I figure I will see a few of them again when I arrive at Stehekin and gather my own last reload box.

28

PIE AND INVISIBILITY IN STEHEKIN

On day Thirty-Nine, Wednesday, September 5, I shuffled slowly and painfully over the Agnes Creek trailhead bridge and waited for the next shuttle bus to arrive, take my five bucks, and transport me the twelve miles down the dusty, bumpy road to Stehekin, situated on the most northern tip of Lake Chelan. While I waited, five other PCT hikers straggled down the trail, and we all sat together under an enormous fir tree by the river. We were a motley bunch with little to say to one another. I think we had used up most our strength to get to that point. I had just completed several days of hiking in a Zen-like silence and didn't feel inspired to talk about anything to anyone. I think there was a tacit agreement among us that silence was perfectly acceptable, and there wasn't much to say. We all had aches and pains and worries and concerns. It wasn't as if we were being unfriendly or uncivil; it was simply that small talk at that point didn't feel appropriate. The quiet didn't need to be filled with chatter.

Stehekin is accessible only by boat, floatplane, horseback, or hiking, and though remote and isolated, it was as welcome a sight as any town or city I had ever visited. And it had everything I wanted or needed: hot coin-showers, free camping sites along the lake, a small general store, a restaurant, a coin laundromat, a post office, and best of all, the most amazing bakery I'd ever encountered. Over the next two days, I would enter that holy of holy place several times for one tasty treat after another.

The area with free camping sites was about a quarter mile from where the shuttle bus dropped us off. I headed there straightaway. I figured if I didn't find something soon, there might not be any spaces left. As it turned out, I was correct, and I did lay claim to the last spot. It was fairly rocky and uneven, but only about twenty feet from the shore of the lake. I quickly set up my tent and emptied my backpack.

Nearby, I met a young woman camping who was waiting for her husband and three of his friends to arrive. They were thru hikers from Vermont, and she had traveled the long distance from her hometown to this tiny hamlet to meet up and accompany them for the last eighty miles to Canada. They were among the last group of thru hikers that had started at the California/Mexico border. Later thru hikers would be hazarding the possibility of bad weather or some of the fires that had started several miles south of us. Someone had told me that a few of the PCT hikers had to vacate the trail on orders from the local rangers. By my calculations, I missed that drama by about four days.

After our conversation, I headed to the village some three hundred yards down the road. When I returned to my campsite about a half hour later with my reload box from home, I gave her one of the oranges Carla had included in my box. In return, she lent me her rented bicycle so I could pedal to the bakery a mile-and-a-half distance for a fresh piece of pie a la mode. It was a perfect trade. I had met various PCT hikers who praised the bakery in Stehekin, and within seconds of entering the front door, I knew I had not been fooled. I stood in the middle of the room, closed my eyes, and deeply inhaled. I had just entered heaven. It was, at least, the most amazing bakery here on earth, set amidst tall cedar trees, outfitted with a quaint, homey dining area, and exuding the aroma of freshly baked breads and pies and cookies and freshly baked pizzas.

I scanned the room and noticed several other PCT hikers I recognized. All of them had plates piled high. Within minutes I, too, had a plate covered with pie and ice cream. I found a table by a window so I could look out at the trees, sip freshly brewed coffee, and begin my sensual encounter with the most delicious piece of raspberry and nectarine pie I had ever tasted. I was so content, I was actually giggling to myself. To someone watching, I probably appeared to be some demented old man who had lost his mind. I finished my pie, ordered a piece of apple-rhubarb pie to go, and bought a fresh brownie as a gift for the woman who had lent me her rented bicycle.

***

Within the first few hours at Stehekin, I decided to take two zero days. The place was just too pleasant to leave. Besides, I needed time to wash my laundry, stay off my aching toe, enjoy a couple of long hot showers, and take time to recover from the arduous (and often scary) hundred-mile hike across the Glacier Peaks Wilderness. I had no reason to rush back on the trail. I had ample time to make it to Harts Pass in time to meet Carla in Winthrop, a small town about thirty miles east of the Pass. And besides, I was enjoying my beautiful camping spot next to the lake and all the surrounding scenery. I also wanted to make a few more bike trips to the bakery! It was a good feeling to know that the hardest part of the hike was behind me. I had only fifty miles and a few more days of hiking before I could claim I had victory.

With the bakery only a ten-minute bike ride away and a restaurant up the road about a quarter mile, it was very tempting to start buying my meals rather than cooking up the supplies I had brought. They were certainly not as enticing or tasty as the former, but my cheaper and more practical self compelled me to eat what I had packed or what had come in my reload box. I limited my bakery runs to just pie and coffee.

After I'd fixed breakfast at camp on the first morning in Stehekin, I walked to the small coffee stand up the road from my campsite and bought a latte. With my freshly brewed coffee in hand, I was sitting on the deck of the restaurant looking out at Lake Chelan, watching the boat (Lady of the Lake) arrive with a group of passengers disembarking for a day in town. Seated next to me was a young man with a full beard grown during his thru hike. He was indulging in his first "breakfast beer." His term. "Jeremiah Johnson" had taken a leave of absence from his work back east to hike the entire PCT. We were engaged in some conversation about his work when two women from the boat took seats at the table next to ours with coffees in their hands. They were in their forties and obviously not equipped for even a day hike. They had come for the trip up the lake and a day in Stehekin then planned to take the next boat in about three hours to return to the town of Chelan.

One of the women looked over at us and asked Jeremiah if he were hiking the PCT. He told them he was and they began a long conversation about his trail exploits. They appeared fascinated by the whole idea of hiking for weeks and months in the wilderness, sleeping on the ground, cooking meals on a small camp stove, and facing all the challenges of a PCT hike. Now, mind you, during this entire interchange between Jeremiah and the two women, Jeremiah and I were sitting together, both wearing our grubby hiking attire, looking the worse for wear. After about a half an hour the women left, Jeremiah turned to me and started to laugh.

"So when did you become invisible?" he asked.

"Oh, about age sixty. Funny you noticed. Most people your age don't."

"Shit, what you did is a whole lot more impressive than what I've done. I could never do what you did. I've been hiking with a group of guys the entire Trail, but you've done it solo." He paused, took a long swig of his beer. "And...well, don't be offended...but someone your age just doesn't do what you did. Shit, you're older than my father!"

"I'm probably older than your grandfather!" I added with a laugh. "It's one of the sad truths about our culture, that older folks become invisible. Ask any woman who goes into a restaurant or store and asks for service. The young, drop-dead beautiful usually get first notice. It's not anything I lament. It's just something I take note of."

"Well, I think it sucks."

"Me too. So don't be a part of it."

We sat looking out at the lake. Him sipping a beer and me a latte. Jeremiah broke the silence.

"So, did your people back home tell you to not attempt this at your age? I mean, why are you doing this?"

I didn't respond right away but sat for a half minute with the question floating around in my mind.

"Maybe being in the wilderness is another way for me to be seen by others as someone having worth. Back home I'm just another retired, old, white-haired guy who used to work somewhere at something. But here in the wilderness, I'm a PCT hiker just like all the others. We're all covering the same miles and experiencing the same wonder and beauty. No matter my age, I share that with everyone else. So I guess I'm here because I *can* be. At my age, a person doesn't put off too long what can or should be done."

Jeremiah was smiling. "Damn, that's one hell of a way to look at it. I got to write some of this shit down and share it with my dad. I got to get his ass out on the trail. Well not here, but sure as hell back home along the AT."

I got up to order another latte, and when I returned a few minutes later, Jeremiah had left. I suspect he caught the afternoon shuttle to the trailhead. He had told me earlier in our conversation that he was on a strict schedule to reach Canada and return home to begin a new job. He had already been gone for nearly five months. He was broke and needed to pick up where he'd left off. I didn't see him again.

I sat on the deck at one of the picnic tables looking out at the blue, serene lake. There were a couple of other PCT hikers sitting nearby, but I didn't feel like starting up a fresh conversation about my hike or theirs. I brought out my journal to capture a few thoughts.

Journal Entry:
Unexpected that Jeremiah took enough interest to ask me about my thoughts and motivations on the PCT. If we had spent more time, I would have told him that I mostly took on this challenge because as long as I can remember, I have had a strong and mystical connection with the out-of-doors. That I love being in the wilderness and especially

being there by myself. Over the course of nearly sixty years I have shared many backpacks with friends and family members, but there is something deeply satisfying to experience the rawness of the wilderness on my own with no distractions and no one else's agenda.

I think Jeremiah understood the thing about invisibility. He actually brought it to my attention. Being seen enables a person to claim their lives and meaning. I'm not certain when that insight became a part of my own self-awareness, but it did occur.

The ironic thing about this phenomenon of invisibility is that it is a secret loss, one we either refuse to acknowledge or speak about. Some are simply unaware that such a fate has befallen them while they quietly go about their lives.

I'm unclear why being invisible to a couple of twitty women visiting Stehekin bugged me. But it is another piece of anecdotal evidence in support of my theory of invisibility. Anyway, the trail teaches a person many things. For me, it continues to teach me a sense of place and perspective and to keep my sense of humor ready at all times.

I do hear complaints of men and women my age who speak about their world getting smaller as they age. Their lives have shrunk and they feel limited. I reject that position. I think a person's world is as small or large as they choose it to be. Being on the PCT is part of my choice to make my world larger. My pace is snail-slow, but I walk and I'm doing what I love doing. "Here I am, world. An old man limping along, slowly, steadily, with determination. I exist!"

I had been sitting in one spot for about a half hour, focused on writing in my journal, when a floatplane came roaring towards the shore and disrupted the tranquility. I watched as it taxied towards the dock, shut off its noisy engines, its two propellers coming to a complete stop. I saw three people cautiously emerge from the plane, set their feet on the bobbing dock, and walk towards the restaurant. I grabbed my latte off the table and headed towards my campsite. I didn't want to talk with more strangers.

29

SIGNAGE, SIGNAGE, MY KINGDOM FOR SIGNAGE

Often I had conversations in my head about what bugged me most about the PCT. Hiking for eight to twelve hours a day allowed ample time to stew about what was amiss in the universe. Most of the time I chose not to let my thoughts drift towards such negativity. Nothing good ever came from it. But from time to time, and mile to mile, I would find myself pondering something that drove me this side of nuts. I had fine-tuned a Top Five List, but from one day to next it shifted, so nothing was ever set in stone. Campers who didn't abide by the Leave No Trace Rule always made the list of top five things that most irritated me.

Another among the Top Five annoyances was the inconsistency or total absence of signage. There were times when I could see a PCT marker a hundred yards from the one I had just passed, but then there were times when I would hike for miles and not see a single sign. There were times when there were side trails and spur trails that could easily be confused as the PCT and I would have to remove The Rock, walk around for a while, check my maps several times, then pick a trail, hoping it was the correct one. Some signs had deteriorated so much that they had actually fallen on the trail itself. I would have to discern if the fallen sign was pointed in the right direction. In some places, someone had taken a pencil or pen and actually written on a PCT sign what direction to take because the sign itself was so ambiguous.

I realized that those who carried a GPS were less likely to experience the same difficulties as someone hiking with only maps as their guides. And as for maps, well, there was an ongoing debate about which was the most accurate and helpful. It warmed the cockles of my heart when I encountered someone who was as confused as me but had all the resources of their downloaded maps and GPS contraptions. Sometimes, an adequate map aided by experience and common sense trumped technology. Nevertheless, I constructed at least two bitchy letters in my mind to send to the PCT Association pleading for a more concerted effort to fix the signage problem. The problem reached its nadir on the afternoon of Day Forty-One.

The previous night I had camped at Nine Mile Camp, about eleven miles from Stehekin. I had decided to leave a day earlier than planned, because I had become weary of all the chatter around my campsite when the thru hikers had arrived and were celebrating their achievements. Their presence was more noise than I could tolerate. I was also feeling rested, and my foot felt less painful. It seemed a good time to leave, so I caught the 8:00 a.m. shuttle to the trailhead.

On the way out of town, the shuttle stopped at the bakery, so the five of us on the bus scampered out and into the holy of holies. The girl at the counter informed us that a Trail Angel had set up an account for all the PCT hikers that paid for one item per person! The blessings never ceased! I chose a very large chocolate chip cookie, as well as a couple apple tarts and a cinnamon roll, all baked just hours before we arrived. So, with bags stuffed with freshly baked goodies and freshly brewed coffee to go, we five returned to the shuttle bus for the twelve-mile ride to the PCT trailhead adjacent to the High Bridge Ranger Station next to Agnes Creek.

The mood of the group was serene and pensive. I didn't know if it was that we were all sleep-deprived, quietly eating our treats, or just thoughtfully awaiting what lay ahead for the next leg of the PCT. For me, there was always a feeling of wonder at the unknown to come. I enjoyed the quiet and stared out the window into a beautiful morning, where the sunlight flickered through the thick foliage. Small talk among us seemed inappropriate.

***

About eleven miles from Agnes Creek, I stopped for the day at Nine Mile Camp. There was nothing significant about that experience, and like many past days, it was a day of unrelenting and difficult elevation gains. I pitched my tent next to a roaring creek, ate a quick dinner, and climbed in to write in my journal before ending the day.

Journal Entry:
Two women from Seattle are camped at the other end of the camp area about fifty feet away. They are camping for a couple of nights out of Rainy Pass. The one was very friendly and seemed to enjoy our short visit until her partner arrived from a wood search. She was quite unfriendly and even annoyed, as if I were going to steal her partner and whisk her off to my tent for the night. The friendly one is a writer who knows some of the places on Whidbey that I do. Has been to Hedgebrook to write. We could have shared more, but her girlfriend was making obvious noises of annoyance, so I thanked them for their hospitality of sharing the campsite and went back to my area. I think this is the first time since I left the Gorge that I have encountered anyone as unfriendly as that particular woman.

I'm going to make an attempt to leave at first light in the morning so I can get to Rainy Pass by noon. It's nearly a 2,000-foot elevation difference, so the hiking will be a long morning of up and up and up!

Besides, I don't want to encounter that grumpy woman again. She's definitely not someone I would want to begin my days with!

***

I reached Rainy Pass at Highway 20 around noon. It was a difficult eight miles. I began the morning at 3,130 feet, and Rainy Pass was at 4,865 feet. It was time for a reasonable break. Not too long but long enough to feel rested. Harts Pass was thirty miles north. I wanted to get as close as possible, which meant I needed to cover about eight more miles, making it a near sixteen-mile day. My toe was killing me, so I wasn't confident I could hike an entire day. I would go as far as the pain allowed. By this time, I could barely get my foot into my boot. It would be a very slow ending to the trip. There were times during the painful miles that I would laugh out loud at my good fortune: Better this had happened to me now than the start of my trip. It was clear that I couldn't hike another hundred miles on this foot, no matter how determined or bull-headed I could get. My body was shouting out a clear message!

I found a spot under a large cedar tree near the outhouse, the only shady area away from the cars parked in the direct sun. Again, my lunch consisted of a few handfuls of trail mix, a protein bar, a couple pieces of turkey jerky, and about a half a bottle of water. There was a water fountain at the parking lot, so I wasn't concerned about how much I consumed at this stop. I had my back against a fallen log and my legs spread out over the cool earth. When I put my head back to rest on the log, I fell asleep for about a half hour and awoke with a stiff neck. But the quick nap felt good and I was eager to resume the hike. I strapped on The Rock, filled up with water, and started searching for the trailhead that led to Cutthroat Pass. I walked back towards where I had come off the trail on the other side of Highway 20, but there was no signage or indication of a trail. I walked up and down each side of the parking lot looking for a trail, or a sign, to no avail. I took off my pack and dug out my maps to see if I had missed the obvious.

After nearly five hundred miles and several weeks of hiking, I had gotten fairly skilled at finding trailheads. But now I couldn't find anything that remotely looked like the beginning of the trail. Again, I walked back and forth along both sides of the parking lot and then again looked at the maps. I had left The Rock near where I had eaten my lunch, and I was hoping another PCT hiker would come along to point me in the right direction. But no such person came, and now I was feeling a little worried that I had really messed something up in my calculations. Nothing seemed to make any sense. I was about to head back down when I saw a couple hikers come down the trail where I had come from. By the time I got close enough to ask them where the trailhead was, I saw for myself. It was behind the outhouse! There was absolutely no signage to give directions. It was an obvious trail, so I suspected I was heading in the right direction, but there was nothing to assure me I was on the PCT.

As I walked north on the path, I grumbled to myself, "How hard could it be to put a sign at that spot to let folks know where they are?" Of all the places in the past few days that needed signage, that was the place. I was pissed! And pretty much stayed that way for the next several miles. Now I really had a bitchy letter written in my head.

My annoyance at the lack of signage was eventually dispelled with relief that I was indeed heading in the right direction. I had lost close to an hour of hiking time but, again, little matter. I had time to spare. Actually, the entire hike was about "time to spare." I had witnessed dozens of fellow hikers, both thru and sectional, who were hell-bent to maintain a schedule. Their goals were either legitimate or manufactured. Some actually had to arrive at their destination because of transportation deadlines or family/work commitments. I was in neither of those camps. I was experiencing one of the rare periods of my life when I had no place I had to be at any given time. I suspect there had been other times such as this, but for the most part, I had spent most my life chasing distant goals, illusive opportunities, or impractical yearnings. Most of my life I had failed to live in the moment. I wanted to take full advantage of this opportunity now.

30

THE LAST DAY

The night of Day Forty-One, I camped about a mile south of Cutthroat Pass in a large, flat space. I set up my tent and went in search of firewood around the perimeter. It was easy pickin's, and within a few minutes I had gathered more than I would need. When I heard the distant sound of giggling and a dog barking, I set down my load of wood at my campsite and walked in the direction of the clamor. About two hundred feet from my own campsite, I found two young women out for a three-day backpack. They were squatting on a blanket near their tent playing some card game, with their dog tethered to a nearby tree. Though they were a bit startled to see me come into their camp, they welcomed me to sit with them and talk about my own journey. I stayed for about a half hour, then excused myself to return to my own place to light my campfire and begin preparations for dinner.

I was at nearly 6,000 feet in early September, so the evenings were cooling off considerably. A small campfire felt good at the end of the day. And besides, I could dry my sweat-laden clothing by the flames. I didn't know which way the two women were headed the next morning, but I knew I wanted to get an early start and be at Cutthroat Pass as early as possible to enjoy the early warmth of the sunrise over the distant peaks and to spend some time just sitting and looking out from the pass onto the vast areas below. I stayed up until nightfall, just sitting by the fire, drinking tea, looking out at nothing in particular, and realizing my long trek would soon be completed.

I missed Carla and wanted to see her, but I wasn't that keen on returning to the routine that I had come to call "my life" back home. I had become accustomed to living very minimally in the wilderness with only a pack that carried everything I needed for that day. It seemed like a good way to live one's life, and hiking through incredible beauty in solitude seemed like a good way to spend a day. But in two days this experience would be ending. I wasn't totally ready to relinquish this level of independence and simplicity. Every day had been a new lesson in living with less. But I *was* ready to have a doctor examine my toe and assure me it wasn't going to fall off.

***

The next morning was perfectly clear and crisp, and I arose excited to begin the day early. I prepared a simple meal so I could be on the trail with minimal fuss by 7:00 a.m. The trail began steeply. Cutthroat Pass was about a mile away, but it was a difficult mile with 1,000 feet of switchbacks. But today my pack felt lighter. Perhaps Carla was correct that it would get lighter as I ate my way through the food day after day, or maybe I had grown stronger over the weeks of hiking and what had once seemed nearly unbearably heavy now came in stride. Perhaps it was merely the excitement of having conquered so much over the past several hundred miles—self-doubts, weariness, anxieties, occasional loneliness, short-term bouts with various bodily pains and aches—that I just felt indomitable. Nothing would feel too heavy at that moment.

Cutthroat Pass was glorious! I removed my pack and sat on a large, flat rock, grabbed a sack of trail mix, and looked out towards Cutthroat Lake in the valley below and the towering Liberty Bell Mountain beyond the lake that rose nearly 8,000 feet. The early morning sun was so comfortable and soothing. It felt as though I could sit at that very spot for the remainder of the day. The only sound I heard was my own breathing and a gentle breeze coming up from the valley. It was a moment I wanted to remember and savor, so I slipped off The Rock where I was sitting and sat on the ground with my back to it. I grabbed my journal from the top pocket of my pack.

Journal Entry:

I think today is the day that Carla and Paige are competing in a triathlon. I think it's so great that they are doing it together. I hope it gives Paige an incentive to maintain her program of health.

I think that today is also the day of Cheryl Reed's memorial service at Trinity Lutheran Church. Bill and I have become friends over the past year, and I hope he saw me as a support during a difficult time in his life. He is genuinely a good and decent person and one of several I have come to know and care about at Trinity. I think, more than a faith community, Trinity has become a place of friendship and fellowship. Perhaps a rare place where I feel welcomed and not judged. I really don't know what people actually think about me, but it feels like a safe place for me and Carla. It's another one of those "courage to accept the things I cannot change."

Strange and improbable how life has led me on pathways I never expected to travel. At one point in my life, with a seminary degree and other higher degrees, I imagined my life to be one of successfully engaging in academics or even pastoring a prestigious church. Now my involvement in the academic life is limited to reading a smattering of fancy-pants books and commenting on them for a nanosecond with another person who might give a shit. And church involvement? Well, it's the choir and an occasional service project. "And the first shall become last..." and "Pride cometh before the fall..." And it all came to pass. Never tempt the gods. But I did. And I have paid dearly for it.

But today I feel vital and clean and on a pathway to redemption. I suppose I can wallow in the past. To no good. I'd rather delight in the present. In this very moment, sitting here with a throbbing toe, blisters upon blisters, worn-out boots, weary muscles and bones, pen in hand writing in a journal, I feel alive and blessed. It all feels good and wonderful. I am grateful that my life has brought me to this very moment. I will not allow the past to define me.

Got to get on the trail. I'm about a day and a half from the end, and I want to savor it all. The truth of it is that I will never pass this way again. I will never again lay eyes on these sights, and I will never step foot on this piece of earth again.

I'm on my way.

***

I stopped at Methow Pass for lunch around 1:00 p.m. From Cutthroat Pass to Methow Pass was six miles of ups and downs. This was a beautiful way to spend a morning of hiking. The trail was a zigzag path that led through Granite Pass and views of Upper and Lower Snowy Lakes. Nothing too severe, which was good, given my toe was now at a level eight on the pain scale. Every step reminded me that bodies are not invincible, and mine was rebelling against my will. Mind and body were definitely not in concert with one another.

On this day of painful hiking, I was lucky to be distracted by views of Mt. Hardy, Mt. Arriva, and Fisher Peak. My guidebook indicated that between where I had left in the morning and Harts Pass, about twelve miles north, there was no water source. No streams or creeks or rills or lakes. So I decided to make camp about fifty feet from a gushing creek just short of Glacier Pass. I dropped my pack alongside the trail and walked a few hundred feet farther just to see if there were any other campsites with more space than the one where I had left my pack. No deal. I returned to my small space and set up camp, sans my tent. I decided that, given my good fortune over the past several weeks of perfect weather and no rain or clouds, I would spend my last night "cowboy camping" and leave my tent in my pack. I gathered some wood for a small fire where I would burn the last two pages of my trail guidebook, which I had found useful throughout the entire trek. Each night at each fire, I would burn the pages of that day's hike. It wasn't a matter of discarding unnecessary weight. It was symbolic. And in keeping with my commitment to routine, even on the last night, I gingerly removed my boots and slid into my Tevas and limped down to the stream for some fresh water. It was icy cold, and I stood next to the water and drank about a half-gallon before returning to my site to boil some water for tea and my last dinner of dehydrated food. It was very tasty, but I wasn't going to weep for its absence in my future diet. I was going to miss kneeling down by the side of a stream, planting my face into the cold running water, and drinking until my teeth hurt. Those who have never had the experience of satisfying their thirst in this manner have missed one of life's great gifts.

I was surrounded by enormous cedar trees. The trail was about five feet from where I sat, so I could hear anyone coming north or south long before they appeared. It wasn't until nearly nightfall that I heard someone rattling up the trail towards my direction. They were a couple in their twenties, and when they saw me sitting writing in my journal, they stopped to ask if I knew of any other campsites up the trail. I told them that I hadn't located any, which was why I was crammed into the small space where I was. Otherwise, I told them, they could squeeze in with me.

They were thru hikers from Maryland determined to reach Canada by nightfall the following day—about fifty miles of rugged hiking. By now I had become accustomed to hearing people speak of high-mileage days. During the first few days on the trail, I just dismissed it as boastful. But as my hike continued, it became almost common to meet people who had hiked twenty-five to forty miles in one day. So this couple talking about a fifty-mile day wasn't about boasting. That was simply what they needed to do to meet up with their connection to get back home. We chatted for a few minutes before they went on their way. When I went to the stream after dinner to fetch some water to douse my fire before I myself climbed into my sleeping bag, I found they had snuggled up into a tiny space next to the stream and were already fast asleep. The young man opened his eyes and gave me a quick, friendly nod. I filled my water bottles and retreated to my site. It was the end of a long day, my last full day on the PCT.

***

I arose the next morning too excited to be hungry for breakfast, but common sense and experience prevailed. I knew that if I didn't have something to eat before I began the day, it wouldn't be long before I would simply be too weak and hungry to continue on. So I did my usual routine of boiling water for coffee, drinking a few cups of Tang, and eating yet another bowl of instant oatmeal, which by now was akin to eating damp sawdust. But I forced it down, cleaned up my dishes, packed up my gear, and began the task of wrapping my foot with the remainder of my Moleskin and tape. By now I could barely get my left foot into my boot without nearly biting through my lip with pain. But I had no other option. I had to get my boot on and lace it tightly.

All that accomplished, I was on my way by 7:00 a.m. Within a few feet I was at the creek where the couple had settled in for the night. They were still asleep, and I was tempted to wake them up with the admonishment that they'd better get on the trail if they expected to hike the fifty miles to Canada before the day's end. I let that thought go and crossed over the narrow footbridge.

Within a few hundred feet I began climbing switchbacks. Once again, this was one of the several places where the PCT Association could have been more attentive to trail directions. But as my ongoing good fortune would have it, within the first couple miles of my hike, the young couple I had met the previous night came up behind me and assured me I was headed in the right direction. They too were baffled by the fact that, of all the many places where signage would be helpful, this was a place where it was absent. They passed me as if I were standing still. I didn't see them again.

The morning was crisp, and the dew was still heavy on all the underbrush and foliage, so within minutes my legs were dripping wet. It felt good. Almost as if nature was giving me a cool, quick bath, which, by any standards, I needed.

I loved starting the days as early as possible. I loved the cool air and the quiet. I liked the smell of freshness that diminished as the day got hotter and breezes kicked up dust. But one of the most pleasant and unexpected experiences enjoyed during the early mornings was having my face covered with dewy spider webs still clinging to low branches or taller bushes. Most of the time I couldn't see them, then suddenly my face would be damp and I knew I had just walked through a spider web. It was as if Creation were reminding me that there were still moments of wonder left to enjoy and I needed to pay attention.

All around me were blueberry bushes, and for the first time since I'd left the Gorge, I was a little unsettled to think I might meet up with a mama bear and her cubs gathering berries for their breakfast meal. And the fact was that the farther north I hiked, the greater possibility there was for such an encounter. Early mornings and blueberries were a recipe for bears. So I did what any reasonably cautious hiker would do in that situation: I intermittently blew the whistle attached to my pack strap near my left jaw. When I wasn't blowing on my whistle, I was loudly singing stanzas of hymns and songs I thought I'd long forgotten. Funny how terror can cleanse the fog of memory. If anyone had been watching, they'd wonder who that old man was, lost, deranged, wandering in the wilderness, and singing for all he was worth. Fortunately, no one was in sight. In fact, I encountered no other hikers for the next several hours.

My pace was slower than ever because with every step it felt as though an ice pick were being jammed into my foot. The downhill portions were the most agonizing. Fortunately, this last day was mostly uphill, and for the first time during the entire hike, I actually hoped for as much uphill as possible.

I started the day at about 4,200 foot elevation and for the first six miles climbed a series of switchbacks to 6,900 feet and to where Tatie Peak could be seen in the distance. Gradually I hiked to lower elevations that remained fairly constant at around 6,000 feet until Harts

Pass at 6,200 feet. As in every preceding day for the past six weeks, this day was sunny and clear. When it came to the weather conditions during the entire hike, I'd hit the mother lode.

For the next several miles, I hiked on a shale-laden trail with no cover from the afternoon sun. The trail was a narrow pathway that circled around the edge of a steep mountain. There was little margin for error. Somewhere around noon I met a couple coming from their campsite at Harts Pass for a day hike. They could see me from several hundred feet away and realized I was struggling. We stopped for a few minutes to chat, and they went on their way to find a place to eat lunch before returning to their campsite at the pass. About a half hour later they returned, saying they had decided to scrap their plans for a picnic in order to carry my pack the next few miles to the pass and then drive me the ten miles down to Highway 20 where I could hitchhike to Winthrop. While I was very moved by their generosity and the sacrifice of their own plans, I explained to them that I had come this far without anyone carrying The Rock and I needed to complete the next few miles without assistance, though I gladly accepted their offer for the ride. We parted with the agreement that they would wait for me at the Harts Pass parking area. That encounter of generosity was enough to lift my spirits and take my mind off the pain in my foot. And my pack actually felt a bit lighter. It is a beautiful thing when the kindness of strangers makes life far more manageable and delightful. It was another example of how Trail Angels added a welcome dimension to the experience.

Harts Pass was still about four miles away. It took me nearly three hours to complete the distance. This was definitely the slowest mileage I had thus hiked. Of course that had mostly to do with my foot, but there was a part of me that simply didn't want to finish. In four miles, the backpack trip of my life would be over and I'd be returning home. I was reluctant to conclude this experience. What had simply begun as a grandiose notion to take a very long hike had become a journey of rising endurance and self-confidence. But more to the truth, it had become one of gratitude and faith.

<u>Last Journal Entry</u>:
THE HIKE IS OVER. IT IS FINISHED. I DID IT!

I am sitting on the deck outside the motel room that Carla reserved for us. My sore foot is propped up on the railing. The sun feels warm and good on my face. Carla should be arriving in the next hour or so. I can hardly wait. I feel like a young teen on his second date with the newest love of his life. Except Carla has been the love of my life for the past twenty-five years...though I have not always treated her thus. There's no such thing as "making up for lost time," but there is this moment and I will make this moment matter.

It's too soon to have an opinion about what this all meant: the long hours of walking, the forty-five days of being alone in the wilderness, the simplicity of it all, the separation from family and friends, the generosity of so many Trail Angels, the so-called Trail Magic I experienced at just the right moments, the many fellow PCT hikers who brought laughter, offered advice, and from time to time pointed me in the right direction, the days and weeks of introspection and pondering a life not all that well spent with years spent in a haze of alcohol, the lost opportunities to love, and serve, and be loved.

Maybe all of this doesn't really mean anything very profound. Maybe it simply means I was given the amazing gift of spending several weeks in some of the most dramatic and stunning wilderness areas in the world, and I drank it all in and survived. I was given the rare opportunity to experience weeks of solitude. I was given the gift of time.

Everything is quiet save for the rushing sounds of the river below. I have experienced Eden, and I will soon be reunited with my Eve, who makes everything complete. But I will miss the days of quiet hours. I feel blessed beyond deserving and comprehension.

AFTERWORD

Before I had even completed the final mile of my trek through Washington, I was adamant that I had taken my last long-distance backpack. I couldn't imagine putting myself through such an ordeal again. I had hiked to utter exhaustion with every resource spent, soreness in every bone, an infected big toe, and the loss of nearly twenty pounds. But sometime between that last day on the PCT stumbling towards Harts Pass and when I arrived back home, I was already making mental plans to hike the Oregon section of the PCT, but cautiously guarded those thoughts. By Christmas, though, I had announced my plans for the following summer: I would hike from Northern California through the Oregon section to the Bridge of the Gods, the very place where I had begun my last trek through Washington. To my delight and relief, no one was surprised. In fact, family and friends figured as much. They understood that I was heading towards my seventy-second birthday and encouraged me to "seize the day."

Much like my preparation in 2012 for my hike through the Washington section, I began the serious planning for the Oregon section in early spring, 2013. That meant selecting maps and guidebooks, upgrading equipment, and collecting what foodstuffs I could at that early stage of planning. With the preliminaries accomplished, it was just a matter of when and from which trailhead I would begin. But there was a catch: I wanted to hike *all* of Oregon, but there was no entry point at the border between Oregon and California. I had to decide whether to begin at Seiad Valley, California (about 100 miles from the Oregon border); someplace in Oregon accessible by car, bus, or train; or begin someplace south of Seiad Valley, which would add more mileage to my hike. I chose to begin in Dunsmuir, California, about 250 miles from the Oregon border. It was the only place where public transportation could deliver me close to the PCT. While the actual hiking is as uncomplicated as putting one foot in front of the other, the logistics of a long-distance trek can get progressively complicated.

Unlike the summer of 2012 when Carla delivered me about fifty yards from the trailhead, in 2013 I took the Amtrak to Dunsmuir to begin my trek. The next morning, the owner of the motel where I stayed for the night drove me the five miles to the trailhead. I hiked seven hundred miles in six weeks. Looking back on that decision and that time in California, I would have skipped those miles, taken the train to Merced, and headed straight to Seiad Valley. The long, uphill, dry, dusty miles in that part of California offered nothing in the way of interest or beauty. It was simply a very hot, steep grind. And within the first couple of days, both of my feet were ravaged by blisters. No amount of Band-Aids or Moleskin seemed to help, and blistered feet plagued me almost the entire trip.

The two summers of hiking were much the same in duration and daily experiences. They both had their stunning views of mountain peaks, lush valleys, meadows rich with flowers, streams to cross, clear, cold lakes for swimming, and forests that provided peaceful and protected campsites. Both sections had unending switchbacks that challenged my stamina and commitment. Both required the necessity to wake each morning and begin again a day of hiking and accomplishing a set goal of time and place.

But there were enough differences that brought the Oregon experience into the light of its own uniqueness: There I met up with Peter, the Trail Angel in Washington who, along with his two large dogs, had guided me across a snowfield. We hung out for a couple hours along the trail and retold our shared experience from the previous summer. We had a few laughs over how I kept trying to either lose or kill myself on a snowfield. On the Oregon section, I reached the highest point of the PCT in Oregon or Washington, 7,600 feet, and camped one night at the forty-fifth latitude line, midway between the equator and the North Pole. Most significantly, though, on the Oregon section, I broke my foot.

If I hadn't been so stubborn, I would have hitched a ride to Bend, Oregon, where I could take a bus and return home. But I had only 165 miles to finish what I had started, and a broken foot wasn't going to keep me from completing my goal. Besides, I knew, once home, I would forever regret my decision to quit.

In the spring of 2014, I entered the lottery to hike the John Muir Trail, a 230-mile hike from Yosemite Valley to Mt. Whitney then down another eight miles to the Whitney Portal. My entry was randomly selected, and against several naysayers with more common sense than me, I started another solo trek that began in the Yosemite Valley and went 230 miles south to Mt. Whitney. It took me twenty days.

It was slow and painful going, but glorious as only the California High Sierras can be. I had taken my first backpack in the Sierras when I was a young teenager. Hiking the John Muir Trail was like coming home after nearly six decades. And now, in writing this final sentence, I believe that as long as I am upright and as long as ibuprofen is still manufactured, my hiking days are not over.